HIDDEN IN PLAIN SIGHT

The Other People In Norman Rockwell's America

Jane Allen Petrick

Published in Miami, Florida by Informed Decisions Publishing

www.wisdomforwork.com

ISBN: 9780989260114
Library of Congress Control Number: 2013914325

Note to the Reader

Whether we love his work or hate it, most of us think of Norman Rockwell as the poster child for an all-white America. I know I did. That is, until I took the uncanny journey I share with you in this book. Then I discovered a surprisingly different truth: Norman Rockwell was into multiculturalism long before the word was even invented.

Working from live models, the famous illustrator was slipping people of color (the term I use for the multi-ethnic group of Chinese and Lebanese, Navajos and African Americans the artist portrayed) into his illustrations of America from the earliest days of his career. Those people of color are still in those illustrations. They never disappeared. But the reason we don't know about them is because, up until now, they seem to have been routinely overlooked.

For example, in her book, "Norman Rockwell's People", Susan E. Meyer catalogues by name over one hundred and twenty Norman Rockwell models, including two dogs, Bozo and Spot. But not one model of color is named in the book.

Another case in point? "America, Illustrated", an article written for *The New York Times* by Deborah Solomon, art critic and journalist. In honor of Independence Day, the July 1, 2010 edition of the paper was dedicated to "all things American".

"America, Illustrated" pointed out that Norman Rockwell's work was experiencing a resurgence among collectors and museumgoers. Why? Because the illustrator's vision of America provided "harmony and freckles for tough times." As Solomon put it, Norman Rockwell's America symbolized "America before the fall." This America was, it seems, all sweetness and light. Solomon simply asserts: "It is true that his (Rockwell's) work does not acknowledge social hardships or injustice."

The America portrayed by Norman Rockwell was also, apparently, all white. Seven full-color reproductions of Rockwell's work augment the multi-page *Times* article. The featured illustration is "Spirit of America" (1929), a 9" x 6" blow-up of one of the artist's more "Dudley Doright"-looking Boy Scouts. None of the pictures chosen to illustrate the article includes a person of color.

This is puzzling. As an art critic, Deborah Solomon surely was aware of Norman Rockwell's civil rights paintings. The most famous of these works, "The Problem We All Live With", portrays a little black girl integrating a New Orleans school.

One hundred and seven *New York Times* readers commented on "America, Illustrated": most of them were not happy with the article. Many remarks cited Solomon's failure to mention "The Problem We All Live With". One reader bluntly quipped: "The reporter (Solomon) was asleep at the switch." The other people in Norman Rockwell's America, the people of color, had been strangely overlooked, again.

This book hopes to begin to correct this oversight. It will be an eye opener for everyone who loves Norman Rockwell, everyone who hates Norman Rockwell, and for all those people in between who never thought much about Norman Rockwell because they believed Norman Rockwell never thought much about them. *Hidden in Plain Sight: The Other People in Norman Rockwell's America* is dedicated to those "other people": individuals who have been without name or face or voice for so long. And it is dedicated to Norman Rockwell himself, the "hidden" Norman Rockwell, the man who conspired to put those "other people" into the picture in the first place.

CONTENTS

Prologue

"Finally, someone is looking. . . "
Laura Claridge, Norman Rockwell biographer

A colored man is perched on top of the Statue of Liberty. Norman Rockwell put him there. But for nearly sixty-five years, no one has said a word about him.

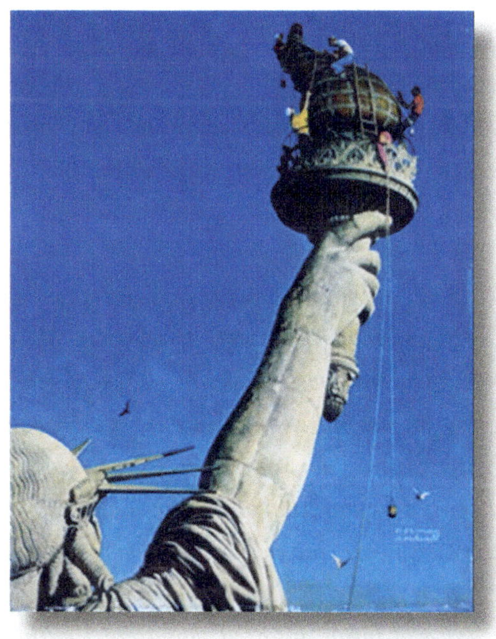

Working on the Statue of Liberty by Norman Rockwell. July 6, 1946

"Working on The Statue of Liberty" appeared as the July 4th, 1946 cover for *The Saturday Evening Post*. The illustration portrays the famous lady being proudly refurbished by five diligent workmen. Three of the workers are white. One of the workmen is a caricature of Norman Rockwell. The fifth worker, the one next to the Rockwell look-alike, is brown.

The model for all of the figures (except the Rockwell look-alike of course) was a white Vermont construction worker named Sousy. Working from photos of Sousy, Norman Rockwell produced a series of charcoal sketches. These drawings reveal that, as "Working on The Statue of Liberty" evolved, Rockwell decided to make a statement about the American experience. He picked up a colored pencil and changed the skin tone of one man from white to brown.

Amazingly, this statement from Norman Rockwell has escaped all notice. The brown man sat unacknowledged on top of Rockwell's Statue of Liberty for sixty-five years before I noticed him while looking for people who looked like me in Norman Rockwell's America. Here's how it all started. . .

ꕥ

October, 2009. Norman Rockwell Museum, Stockbridge, Massachusetts. Final stop of three-day road trip. Given an unseasonably frosty morning and my thinned out blood, I am bundled up like Nanook of the North.

My friend and traveling buddy Pennie Scales (a hardy Yankee farm girl, much more lightly dressed than me) proceeded directly to the main gallery. I, on the other hand, had to stop to de-mummify myself in the coat room. After piling my winter gear into a locker, I headed towards the galleries.

The main corridor of the museum opens onto a large rotunda. Coming out of the coat room into this corridor and looking straight ahead, I could see the circular visitors' desk and beyond that, the back wall of the first gallery.

As I stuffed the locker key into my back pocket, I realized I was alone in the hallway. The visitors' desk was virtually empty as well. But just beyond it, a noisy mass of heads and torsos pulsated, apparently gathering for a museum tour. A huge painting looked down upon the hubbub from the back gallery wall. My eyes moved up to it and I stood stock still.

Over the top of the crowd, left profile facing me, floated a dark brown forehead topped by a thick wooly braid.

My shoulders dropped. My breathing slowed. My lips released a yogic "aa-ahh", curving into a slight smile. I felt great. And I did not have the slightest idea why.

As the tour group surged off with its docent, I moved closer to the painting. Then, there I was, standing right in front of. . . myself! My six-years old, 1950's, Bridgeport, Connecticut self. Skin oiled, socks evenly folded down, white sneakers gleaming. Walking with a straight back the way numerous trips up and down our railroad apartment with Encyclopedia Britannicas on my head had taught me to do. There was my double, striding off to school in Norman Rockwell's painting, "The Problem We All Live With."

The docent and her ducklings were headed my way, so I tacked against the flock to the other side of the room. There I encountered a portrait of a crisply dressed African-American dining car waiter: shoes polished, uniform immaculate, dignity as well as forbearance in the smile he gives his young white customer. That waiter was my Uncle Hugh!

Well, not really. But at that moment, in my strangely-altered state, he seemed to be my Uncle Hugh.

Hugh was my mother's oldest brother. My mother was the third youngest of thirteen children born to a somewhat self-consciously middle class black family in Baltimore, Maryland. Her big brothers were like second daddies to her, and although he died before I was born, my mother often told me stories about this favorite brother. The family was very proud of the fact that Hugh had a job as a Pullman porter, great work for a colored man in those days.

Mommy would reminisce about how sharp Hugh looked in his gleaming Pullman uniform. When he got home from a tour on the trains, Hugh would scoop up his little sister, swing her above his head until she was hysterical with giggles and then, from the deep recesses of his jacket pockets, present her with a rainbow of hard candies. I always felt a special fondness for my Uncle Hugh. And now, here he was, (or at least he seemed to be), smiling out from the Norman Rockwell painting, "Boy in a Dining Car".

Using a dining car from the New York Central's Lake Shore Limited as his setting, Norman Rockwell had captured a moment in his own son Peter's life when he created the December 7, 1946 Saturday Evening Post cover, "Boy in a Dining Car". In the illustration, a young white patron earnestly tries to calculate a tip for the smiling black waiter standing by. Ten year old Peter Rockwell himself was the model for the young patron. Norman Rockwell hired Jefferson Smith, a twenty-eight year veteran employee on the New York Central Railroad, to portray himself as the waiter in the tableau.

I looked up into the waiter's face and smiled. "Hi, Uncle Hugh!" I whispered. "How you doin?" Then that strange feeling of relaxation flowed over me again. And this time, I knew why.

Traditionally (at least among those of us who were raised right), when one African American encounters another in a situation where we are few, some gesture of acknowledgement occurs. A head nod. Eye contact and a slight smile. A soft, "How you doin'?"

Standing in this gallery of the Norman Rockwell Museum, I realized that I had had no such interaction for three days. In all the historic sites I had visited, all the trails Pennie and I had hiked, all the gift shops we had browsed, coffee shops in which we had gossiped, in all that time and all those places, I had not seen nor been greeted by one other black person.

Now I am very used to being "the only one." A la *Ralph Ellison in his book,* The Invisible Man, *I have internalized my own invisibility. So three days in the Berkshires with no other black people around was not startling. What was startlingly was stumbling upon a clear presence of me and my friends and my family, thanks to Norman Rockwell!*

❦

Erin McLauglin, a blogger on "Teaching Digital History," observes that, on the surface, "Boy in a Dining Car" appears to be a coming-of-age narrative. However, she continues, the work holds much deeper interpretations: "(The porter views) the young boy with compassion and patience. In this way, it is the African American man (who has the) confidence and power and in turn, he is using his power to give respect and compassion (back) to the young boy."

Respect, compassion and patience: that was my Uncle Hugh. And Norman Rockwell had captured it all.

My mind reeled. Norman Rockwell, icon of white-on-white America, had created portrayals of black people that rang very true to me as a black person.

The docent was now concluding her tour, heading back into the gallery in which I stood. Concluding her remarks, she commented that all of Rockwell's portrayals were drawn from live models. "Including the people of color?" I turned and asked her. "Yes," she replied, "including the people of color."

Questions flew around in my head. Who were these "colored" models? Where had Norman Rockwell found them? What had been the quality of their experiences with the famous illustrator? And why had Rockwell chosen to depict them at all?

Standing in front of my "Uncle Hugh" that chilly October morning, I decided to go and find out.

Chapter 1

EARLY GLIMPSES

Colored people were *the* topic of conversation in Norman Rockwell's Vermont during the spring of 1946. And those conversations were not always pleasant.

In March of that year, Crystal Malone, a 19-year-old junior at the University of Vermont, Burlington, had been accepted as a pledge to the *Upsilon* chapter of *Alpha Xi Delta* sorority. Malone, a native of Washington, D.C., was black. *Alpha Xi Delta*, founded in 1893 in Galesburg, Illinois, had been, up until Miss Malone's pledge, all white.

When Crystal Malone arrived as a freshman at UVM in 1943, there was only one other black student on campus. Having grown up in and been conditioned by the segregated world of Washington, Crystal never expected to be asked to join a white sorority. She was pleasantly shocked when she was.

Alpha Xi Delta's invitation to Crystal may have been one of the outcomes of a conference held at UVM the previous November. Anti-Semitism and "anti-Negroism" were its themes. According to "The Cynic," the UVM school paper, when the conference ended, one hundred students "thronged the lounge to elect a committee to investigate the quota system and abolish it on this campus."

The committee met with quick success in several areas. In January, 1946, "The Cynic" proudly announced, "Henceforth, all sorority rushing will be on a basis of no racial or religious discrimination."

Interviewed about the matter decades later, Crystal Malone Brown recalled, "When I was asked to join *Alpha Xi Delta*, I remember being pleased—the spoken emotions and feelings after the war (World War II) made me think it was possible."

But it wasn't. When *Upsilon* Chapter announced that it had pledged Crystal Malone, *Alpha Xi Delta* national president, Beverly Robinson, immediately traveled from Washington, D.C. to Burlington. Her mission: convince the black co-ed not to go through with the pledge. Sitting in a student lounge, Mrs. Robinson advised Malone, "Life is selective, and maybe it's just as well to learn it while we are young."

Crystal Malone declined to be de-selected. *Upsilon* chapter vowed to stand by their colored pledge and ushered her into full sisterhood–at which point the national office of the sorority suspended the UVM chapter.

The women of *Upsilon* chapter appealed to the university administration for help. But university President J.S. Millis was somewhat wishy-washy concerning the controversy. According to "The Cynic," the president's response was, "This is a matter between the local sorority and the national." The campus, and a good part of the state of Vermont, was thrown into an uproar.

UVM faculty and students staged massive protests, overwhelmingly in support of the young sorority women of *Upsilon* chapter. *Life* magazine sent a crew up to Burlington to cover the story, complete with photographs of Malone, a quintessential co-ed in pearls and cashmere. In the article, "Sorority Fight: Vermont Chapter Stirs Nationwide Controversy by Admitting Negro", published May 20, 1946, the magazine smugly observes, "Last winter *Life* pointed out that sororities were undemocratic."

Throughout Vermont, letters to the editor poured into local newspapers, some in support of the *Upsilon* chapter coeds, many, with nasty racial epithets, against them. Letters poured into the office of President J.S. Millis as well, the majority of them urging him to take a strong stand in support of Crystal Malone and her soon-to-be sorority sisters. One of those letters was from one of Vermont's most famous citizens: Norman Rockwell.

Norman Rockwell hated bigotry. Decades later, he would tell *Esquire Magazine*, "I was born a white Protestant with some prejudices which I am continuously trying to eradicate."

Rockwell's rejection of those prejudices was one of the many reasons he wasn't close to his only sibling, Jerry. Jerry's incessant racist jokes infuriated Rockwell. But the venom that the illustrator had witnessed oozing forth when news broke about a colored girl pledging *Alpha Xi Delta*? That had been worse than anything he had ever heard from Jerry.

And so Rockwell, along with his wife Mary and their friends John and Dorothy Canfield Fisher, sent UVM President J.S. Millis a statement of outrage and support: outrage at the prejudice being displayed and support for those standing up against it. The famous illustrator wanted to be sure the letter showed Malone and those spunky sorority girls that Norman Rockwell was proud to stand with them.

But President Millis did not step in and the national office of *Alpha Xi Delta* did not back down. So the sorority sisters of *Upsilon* Chapter, including Crystal Malone, who had completed her pledge and "gone over," performed an historic act of protest: they burned their sorority charter. Doing so meant that no UVM group, including themselves, could use the name *Alpha Xi Delta* for five years. Knowing this, the chapter decided to close its doors, essentially saying: "if we can't be *Alpha Xi Delta* with Crystal, there will be no *Alpha Xi Delta*."

Crystal Malone went on to graduate as a business major with the Class of 1947 and to marry Wesley Brown, the first African-American graduate of the US Naval Academy at Annapolis. In 2008, the National Office of *Alpha Xi Delta* sought out Crystal Malone Brown, wishing to offer her a formal apology. As Deanna Detchemendy, then national president of the sorority recounts:

> *When I contacted Mrs. Brown's daughter (Carol Jackson) with the hopes of getting in touch with Mrs. Brown and arranging a meeting at which* Alpha Xi Delta *would formally apologize, she shared that Mrs. Brown had generally conveyed positive memories of her relationship with* Alpha Xi Delta *to her children, most particularly of her* Upsilon *Chapter sisters who were so very supportive. And that while certainly difficult, she (Mrs. Brown) perceived the incident with our then-national officers as one that helped shaped her character in positive ways as an adult.*

Detchemendy went on to say that:

Mrs. Brown was not in good health, and Mrs. Brown had been diagnosed with Alzheimer's disease and was experiencing (and would continue to experience) related mental deterioration. Given this information, we felt that outreach to Mrs. Brown at that point and the related dredging of negative memories could easily cause more harm than good at this stressful time for the family, and so we determined to forego "closure" on our end in order to avoid opening old wounds for Mrs. Brown or her family.

Crystal Malone never modeled for Norman Rockwell. But photos in *Life* magazine confirm that, with her saffron-colored skin and long, silky tresses, Crystal could have portrayed Spice Mackson. Spice is the key figure in "Love Ouanga," Rockwell's illustration of a black Pentecostal congregation for a short story of the same name.

"Love Ouanga"

"Love Ouanga", written by Kenneth Perkins, appeared in the June, 1936 issue of *American Magazine*. Set in 1930's New Orleans, the story is a beautiful and rich reprise of *La Traviata*, but this time with a happy ending. And this time, the characters are all black.

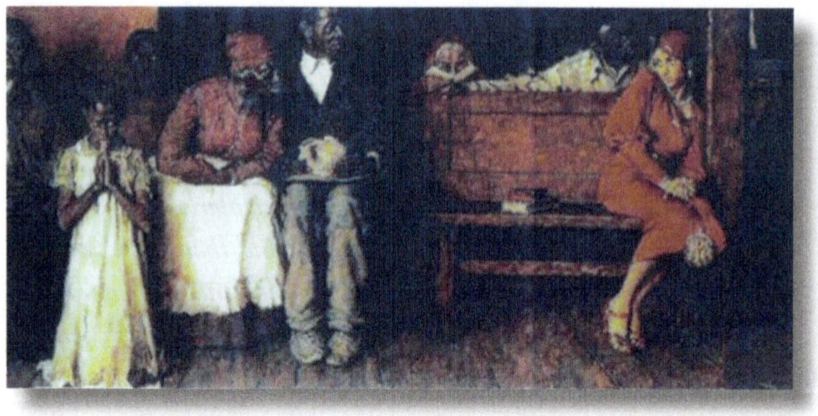

Love Ouanga **by Norman Rockwell. June, 1936**

ᔓᔕ

Spice Mackson lives in a better, although not the best, part of black New Orleans, her simple cabin serving as a beauty parlor by day and a love nest for hire by night. Only two people hold the center of Spice's love. The first is her baby boy, "one of the gods, a little one, but as real as ever her ancestors had worshipped in Guinea": a little god, yes, but one who needs a poppa. The second is Tad Barley, scion of a prominent black New Orleans family, who is ready and willing to fill that need and marry Spice: lock, stock and baby.

The fly in the ointment is Tad's father, Aesop Barley. A powerful precinct boss who speaks in the affected cadences of "the educated negro," Barley Senior confidently opines that his degrees from Tuskegee Institute and Howard University have basically taken most of the African out of him. When he hears of his son's plans to marry Spice, Aesop Barley immediately enrolls Tad in a Negro Officers' camp in Iowa and prepares to ship him out.

Balking at the plan, Tad slips over to Spice's place and urges her to run away with him. But Spice is determined to stay put. New Orleans is home: her beauty parlor is here, Tad's future law career is here. If they run off, they might end up just being "cotton choppin' Nigras."

While Spice pleads with Tad, Aesop Bradley approaches Spice's home. Tad sneaks out the back door as Aesop enters the front with a policeman, a social worker and a court order to take away the baby. The order stipulates that if Spice leaves town and stays out for three years, the child will be returned to her.

The mother's wails bring neighbor women swarming into the cabin. They offer her water but she asks for, and gets, gin. When the commiserating assembly then asks Spice what she plans to do, she responds, "I'm goin to a prayer meeting."

ᔓᔕ

The congregation of "Blood of The Lamb" church consisted of thirty decidedly down-and-out black folks worshiping in a decidedly down-and-out part of New Orleans. One member of this flock, however, was very well known, revered, and at times feared, in all parts of town. Her name was Swamp Suzanne.

Swamp Suzanne, although a dedicated participant in the energetic Christian worship of "Blood of the Lamb," was also a powerful voodoo priestess. Her praying could flip from the God of Israel to the gods of Guinea in a heartbeat. Suzanne's ability to assemble *ouangas*, compilations of rituals and potions that hypo-charged her prayers, was legendary. Spice Mackson headed straight down to the Wednesday night prayer meeting of "Blood of the Lamb." She intended to get Swamp Suzanne "to pray for old Barley a whole lot."

When Spice arrives at the church and slouches to the end of a bench, forgetting to throw away her cigarette, the entire congregation gaps at her. Here was a "city gal sho' nuff." It is this moment Norman Rockwell captures in "Love Ouanga."

ඏ

"Love Ouanga" ends well. When Swamp Suzanne hears that Aesop Barley has stolen Spice's baby, she enlists the assistance of the rest of the congregation in assembling an *ouanga* to put on him. Spice, frightened that the spell might actually kill Barley, runs out to warn him. But a drumming in his head (along with the phone call he received from a church member informing him that he was about to be voodoo-ed) had already drawn Aesop Barley, half-crazed, to the church building.

The congregants see him coming and flee, abandoning the artifacts of the ceremony. But Spice stays behind, and through various ploys with the *ouanga* implements, convinces Barley Senior that if her baby is returned, she can lift the spell. He agrees; she does; and all live happily ever after. "It was not a hate *ouanga* she had worked," Barley muses to himself as he watches an exhausted Spice stagger back to her cabin to welcome her baby and Tad. "It was a love *ouanga*."

Reactions to Rockwell's Illustration of "Love Ouanga"

Reproductions of "Love Ouanga" appear in a number of Rockwell anthologies, but never within the context of Kenneth Perkins' story. Presented without that context, the picture elicits reactions ranging from bafflement to embarrassment to downright offense.

For example, I showed "Love Ouanga" to several black Rockwell models without their knowing the story behind the painting. When I mentioned that I was considering using this illustration as the cover of my book, their recoil from the idea was as obvious as that of the congregants of "Blood of the Lamb" to Spice.

Yet "Love Ouanga" affirms Rockwell's magical talent for telling stories with paintings as much as any *Saturday Evening Post* cover. The blacks in "Love Ouanga" are not the caricatures typical of 1930's portrayals of blacks, nor do they all "look alike": each is uniquely rendered. In fact, the art critic Karal Ann Marling asserts that Spice Mackson is the most beautiful woman Norman Rockwell ever painted.

The striking figures in "Love Ouanga" range from coal-black to saffron yellow: it is reasonable to assume that the models from whom they were drawn had skin shades spanning the same palette. And those models probably came from the very historic black community residing in New Rochelle, New York.

In 1936, the year he painted "Love Ouanga," Norman Rockwell's home was New Rochelle. He had moved there from New York City with his parents in 1913. By 1936 he had married and divorced his first wife, Irene, and was now living with his second wife, Mary and their three sons.

A community sitting on Long Island sound about twenty miles north of the Bronx, New Rochelle was settled in 1688 by French Protestants. These Huguenot artisans fled to New York (then called New Amsterdam) by way of the Caribbean, bringing blacks from the islands north with them. By the late 1700's, a significant number of people of African descent, both slave and free, were living in New Rochelle.

For example, the first national census, taken in 1790, shows New Rochelle with a nearly 20% black population: 136 of its 692 residents were African-American. The 1820 census shows 150 African-Americans residing in New Rochelle. Only six of them were slaves.

A prominent Quaker couple, James and Mary Mott, had much to do with the pre-Civil War absence of slavery in New Rochelle. In July, 1776, the Motts purchased mill property on the shore of Long Island Sound. There, in 1801, they build Premium Mill, the country's largest flour mill at the time.

The Motts' oldest son James, also a Quaker and a staunch abolitionist, was the husband of Lucretia Coffin Mott, a founder of the American Anti-Slavery Society (and a champion of the woman's suffrage movement). The Mott family home in New Rochelle is believed to have been a station on the Underground Railroad.

By 1936, New Rochelle boasted a vibrant African-American community. Black stores, restaurants, funeral parlors abounded. Norman Rockwell would have had little trouble finding colored models for "Love Ouanga." A stickler for veracity, it is highly likely the illustrator even visited several of the historic black churches in his home town, just to get the picture right.

However, when the Rockwell family moved to Arlington, Vermont in 1939, finding models of color became more of a challenge.

Looking for Color in Arlington, Vermont

Vermont is the whitest state in the union. Presently, only 2% of Vermont's population is non-white.

But this has not always been the case. One hundred-and-fifty years before Norman Rockwell went looking for colored models in the Green Mountains, the town of Vergennes, Vermont was 7% black. In the early 1800's, the Vermont communities of Braintree, Winsor and Burlington were each over 3% black. And these were free people of color: slavery had been outlawed by the state's constitution in 1777.

In her book, *Discovering Black Vermont*, Elise A. Guyette asserts that the myth of an "always white" Vermont emerged out of historians' need to focus on research topics having valid, accessible documentation. Believing that African-Americans had never been a presence in Vermont, historians did not look for documentation of their existence there.

Vermont, however, from the Federalist period until the Reconstruction era, was home to numerous free black families peacefully maintaining their small farms. Many became integral parts of their integrated communities, holding public office and serving on church boards.

For example, Lemuel Haynes, born to a white mother and a black father in 1753, was raised as an indentured servant in the home of a pious Puritan church deacon. Haynes went on to become one of the most influential Calvinist ministers in New England, serving as pastor to Rutland, Vermont's West Parish Church for thirty years. He was the first black pastor of a white congregation in the United States. In 1804, Middlebury College granted Lemuel Haynes an honorary degree, the first honorary degree bestowed upon a black American.

But after passage of "The Fugitive Slave Act" in 1850, the history of the "real Vermonter" began to whiten. The reason? The emergence of the theory of "scientific racism".

Scientific racism purported that blacks and whites have different genetic origins. This erroneous doctrine supported the claim to inalienable rights for whites while buttressing belief in the ineradicable inferiority of blacks, just as newly-freed people of color were seeking the full advantages of democracy. Combined with the "Fugitive Slave Act," scientific racism produced a cloud of suspicion around anyone brown. It was no longer comfortable to be colored in Vermont.

So, colored people began to "disappear". They disappeared, not through migration, but through marriage. One hundred years of living together in small, integrated farming communities had resulted in a large mixed race population. Now, increasingly, these colored Vermonters called themselves "white" and sought white spouses for themselves and their children. By the time Norman Rockwell moved to Arlington in 1939, all the native black Vermonters had vanished. If he wanted to depict people of color in a painting, he was going to have to look some place else for the models.

❧

1942: Americans were in the grip of World War II and things were not going well. Norman Rockwell wanted to present his "The Four Freedoms" paintings as bold statements of tolerance and hope, values that were under deadly attack "over there."

Rockwell worked on the four posters for seven months. Wrestling with "Freedom of Worship" took two of them. In "Freedom of Worship," the artist was trying to portray two complex subjects in one painting: racial tolerance and religious freedom.

Rockwell's first attempt at putting these concepts onto a canvas was set in a country barbershop. Initial sketches show a Jew, a Negro and a Catholic priest harmoniously hanging out together while waiting to be groomed by a white, "obviously" Protestant barber.

These initial sketches satisfied Rockwell. But Catholic friends who saw the drawings said, "Priests don't look like that." And WASP associates really didn't recognize the barber as an Episcopalian (or as a Presbyterian, for that matter).

Then there were the opinions of the black people who passed through West Arlington for various reasons: Evelyn Hardy, for example, housekeeper to neighbors up the road. As far as this group of critics was concerned, the Negro's skin was much too light. . . or much too dark. Rockwell's whole initial concept for "Freedom of Worship" fell apart.

After much angst, however, the artist finally came up with another conceptualiztion. "Freedom of Worship" portrayed people of different faiths and different ethnicities, all in an attitude of worship. Evelyn Hardy, the neighbor's housekeeper, was asked to model as one of them. She appears as the thoughtful black woman in the upper-left-hand corner of the painting.

For Hardy, posing as a Rockwell model was one of the most momentous events of her long life. Born in New Jersey, Hardy died there in 1985 at the age of 102. In a local newspaper article commemorating her centennial, Hardy explains that she met Norman Rockwell in the mid-1940's while working as housekeeper for a wealthy Vermont family who were friends of the illustrator.

Rockwell invited Evelyn Hardy to pose several times, producing numerous sketches of her full face and profile. Hardy was paid the standard modeling fee: $10 per sitting. However, the famous illustrator also gave her a memento that turned out to be far more valuable: a sketch of herself drawn in 1943, the year his studio burned down. The sketch was signed, "To Mrs. Evelyn Hardy from Norman Rockwell."

Evelyn Harding treasured this personal keepsake, holding onto the sketch as long as she could. "He (Norman Rockwell) was a wonderful person, a very nice person." However, nearing 98 years old and facing financial difficulties, the aged Rockwell model finally had to part with her signed Rockwell sketch. In 1981, Evelyn Hardy sold her Norman Rockwell portrait to a museum for $4500.

ꟹ

While Norman Rockwell painted the war effort from the bucolic banks of the Battenkill River in rural Vermont, folks in urban Bridgeport, Connecticut worked the war effort in the many industries that boomed along the banks of the Housatonic River. By the time I celebrated my first birthday in April, 1946, my father, William "Buddy" Allen, had leveraged the flood of demand for housing arising from southern black workers seeking some of those good factory jobs into ownership of two pieces of real estate. His second piece of property was our three stories, six family brick home on George Street.

Built in 1914, just at the beginning of World War I, its name, "St. George", was conspicuously carved in the stone above its third story lattice. Over the fifty-one years spanning the building's opening and my birth, its surrounding neighborhood had gone from white Protestant middle class to white immigrant working class. It remained, nevertheless, a white neighborhood.

My dad's first property in Bridgeport had been a rooming house located on "the other side of town", in the basement of which Buddy ran the longest established permanent floating crap game in the state of Connecticut. When he had garnered from these games a large enough stash of cash, my father got his Jewish friend, Ray Blank to front for him on the purchase of the St. George, white tenants and all. Mr. Allen then proceeded to move his new wife and their soon to be arriving first child (me) into his new home. Thus George Street received its first colored residents, (we were colored back then, not black, and certainly not African-American) and its first colored landlord to boot.

Norman Rockwell's Urban Connection

Although his home was rural Vermont, Norman Rockwell knew about integrated urban neighborhoods like 1940's Bridgeport, Connecticut. Long before interstates, Levittown and "white flight," working-class neighborhoods in Troy, New York and Los Angeles, California attracted the artist. He drew sketches and took photographs of their tenements and people. These sketches provided the backdrop for two of Rockwell's *Saturday Evening Post* covers, "Homecoming GI" (1945) and "Road Block" (1949). Both illustrations include people of color.

Troy, known as "The Collar City," was home to Arrow Shirts, whose "Arrow Collar Man" was made famous by advertisements illustrated by Rockwell's mentor, friend and New Rochelle neighbor, J.C. Leyendecker. Troy was a booming factory town, manufacturing four million collars a week during the 1920's. Another source of industrial fame for the town was its ironworks, fabrications that, in the mid-1800's, were second only to those of Pennsylvania.

From his Vermont home, Norman Rockwell frequently traveled through Troy on his way to Albany, New York where he caught the train to New York City. When the artist decided to create a *Post* cover commemorating World War II vets coming back to their home towns, he decided to make that home town working-class Troy, New York.

"Homecoming GI" appeared on the cover of the *Saturday Evening Post* on May 25, 1945. Among the folks gleefully (or shyly, in the case of his young sweetheart) welcoming home the young soldier is not only Norman Rockwell himself (standing in a doorway of the tenement) but also two young boys recklessly hanging from a tree they have climbed, wildly waving a welcome. One of the two boys is black.

In 1945, kids just went out to play: no "helicopter parents," no play dates. Black and white kids frolicked and fought together up and down America's streets. Think "Our Gang."

Elsie Wagner Fenic, in her moving memoir "White Girl in Harlem," provides a lovely glimpse into this time. A second generation Polish-American, Fenic can still jump a pretty mean double dutch, thanks to spending her first nineteen years enjoying 1940's New York City street games with black and Latino friends.

Norman Rockwell put black and white playmates together in "Homecoming GI", not to make a civil rights statement but because, on the streets of Troy in 1945, they were really there. Rockwell's artistic integrity demanded he put them in the picture.

ઌ

The 1940's working class neighborhoods of Troy, New York were a mirror image of my neighborhood in Bridgeport. Just as Troy was known for shirts and iron, Bridgeport was known for brass and bras. Norman Rockwell could have sketched "Homecoming GI" while standing on the corner of my block.

When Mr. and Mrs. Gravina's son, Tommy, came home from the Navy (even though it was with a brown-skinned Puerto Rican wife that talked funny English), the whole neighborhood turned out to welcome him: Italian, Polish, Irish, the several colored families that had moved into Mr. Allen's apartment house (after most, but not all, of the white tenants had moved out). If any of us had subscribed to The Saturday Evening Post *or gone to read it in the library (we didn't), we would have recognized the scene on the May 25, 1945 cover right off the bat. Those boys up in the tree? That was Jimmy Buffalini (the white one) and J.D. Bradshaw (the black one), two of the most rascally devils ever to terrorize a little girl on a tricycle.*

Residents of George Street didn't know much about Norman Rockwell. But looking at "Homecoming GI," it certainly seems like Norman Rockwell knew something about us.

ઌ

Another Norman Rockwell urban setting was Los Angeles, California. During the winter of 1948-49, while vacationing with his in-laws in Los Angeles, Rockwell paid a visit to a Mrs. Merrill, widow and owner of a rooming house for women. The famous illustrator wanted to borrow her entire house.

Located in the MacArthur Park neighborhood of Los Angeles, 719 South Rampart Boulevard was a three-story tenement flanked by similar structures and the "Pacific Telephone and Telegraph" building, the place of work for many of Mrs. Merrill's boarders. Rockwell sought Mrs. Merrill's permission to stage a photo shoot in front of her building. Capturing the street as well as some of its residents as models, he would then use these photos to create one of his famous *Saturday Evening Post* covers. But Mrs. Merrill said no.

Apparently, even back in 1949, not everybody loved Norman Rockwell. The feisty LA landlady felt that, in his paintings, the famous artist did not "enhance" his subjects. Rockwell persisted in his request, however, and Merrill finally gave in: for payment of $50.00.

The camera crew showed up on South Rampart while one of Mrs. Merrill's roomers, Antonia Piasecki, was doing her laundry. In a letter to the Norman Rockwell Museum she writes: "Mr. Rockwell asked me for some fancy undies for the clothes line. I gave him nylon stockings, black lace trimmed panties and bra which he hung up himself. . . ."

A moving truck arrived, complete with California license plates and two moving truck drivers. Lots of photos were taken. The result was "Road Block," the character-filled illustration which appeared as the cover of *The Saturday Evening Post* on July 9, 1949.

Norman Rockwell put himself in the painting: he's the violin teacher looking out the window of what was actually Ms. Piasecki's bedroom. Ms. Piasecki also got to be a Rockwell model: she's the young woman leaning out the window below Rockwell. The red-haired lady standing at the basement door? That's the resister-turned-Rockwell model, Mrs. Merrill.

The models for other figures in the painting have been identified, as well. Joseph Magnani, director of the Los Angeles County Museum of Art and a friend of Rockwell's, is the artist hanging out of the window in a building across the street, accompanied by a barely-draped young lady. Peter Rockwell, the artist's youngest son, is the bespeckled boy with the violin right below them. But Ms. Piasecki does not remember "there being all those children (at the shooting site) at the time."

"All those children" is probably Ms. Piasecki's polite code for the two little black kids posed at the bottom of the scene. They stand solemnly with their backs to the viewer, studying the impasse created when the big red truck meets a little white dog.

Apparently, Norman Rockwell didn't actually encounter any black children on South Rampart Street that day. But given his understanding of similar neighborhoods in Troy, New York (and Bridgeport, Connecticut), he knew they were there, somewhere. So Rockwell went out and found them.

ɞ

They are touching in elegance, innocence and simplicity. Two black children, a little girl and an older boy, in rear profile. The black and white photo in the Norman Rockwell Museum archives shows the boy's shirt crisply pressed, the little girl's braids impeccably arranged. Both are standing holding their hands behind their backs, staring out at an unseen horizon.

That's all I've been able to find out so far about these two little colored models in "Road Block". No names are written on the back of the photo. The meticulously kept Rockwell receipts do not reveal who was paid for posing for this shot. The locale of the photograph, although it appears to have been taken in Los Angeles, is not known for sure, either.

But this is known: in 1949, Norman Rockwell purposely went out and found two black children to model for him so he could place their figures in his illustration. Rockwell knew they were supposed to be in the picture.

ɞ

The house at 7149 South Rampart Boulevard has disappeared. Where the building once stood now stands a parking lot. In the 1950's, integrated neighborhoods began disappearing from America. Correspondingly, colored models disappeared from Norman Rockwell's 1950's paintings as well.

ɞ

But urban or rural, white or black, Americans of every hue joyously celebrated their country's victory over the Axis powers in World War II. When asked to commemorate this celebration on the cover of *The Saturday Evening Post*, Norman Rockwell wanted to portray its multicultural nature. His commitment to realism, even apart from his liberal values, required it.

Expressions of diversity needed to be made subtly, however, subtly enough to get past the censorious eye of *Saturday Evening Post*'s publisher,

George Horace Lortimer. Lortimer discouraged the appearance of people of color in *The Saturday Evening Post*. And when they did appear, he would allow them to be shown only in menial positions.

Rockwell had managed to sneak black kids into "Homecoming GI" and "Road Block." But those were kids. For his painting celebrating America's WWII victory, "Working on the Statue of Liberty," the artist wanted to portray *men*, American men preserving the torch of freedom. And preserving the Statue of Liberty was not a menial job.

So the artist needed a discreet way, an almost clandestine way, to get a colored person into the picture and onto the cover. Rockwell's gambit, when he played it, was so discreet that no one noticed it for over sixty years.

Chapter 2

HIDING IN THE WHITE HOUSE

"From the people with whom we have talked it seems that Rockwell's idea of the symbolism of the torch completely failed to go across".
Report to The Director of the Monument, July, 1946

The year was 1946 and The Statue of Liberty was in trouble. During World War II, neither money, men nor materials existed for the maintenance of the Fair Lady. Now that the freedoms she symbolized had been secured, Lady Liberty herself stood somewhat in jeopardy.

Unseasonably warm weather during the spring of 1946 did not help matters. Fueled with post-war enthusiasm, hordes of visitors, domestic and foreign, sought the balmy breezes of a ferry ride over to Bedloe's Island, home of Lady Liberty. Lieutenant Leonard Spinrad of the New York City Police Department complained to the director of the monument that the statue was dangerously overcrowded, with poor pedestrian traffic control. Adding to the director's woes was continued trouble with the ferry boats. They kept breaking down, stranding large crowds on the island. The director replied to the police lieutenant that, given his small staff depleted by war service, he was doing the best that could be done.

By March, 1946, the Monument's administration knew it would be awhile before post-war money and manpower were loosened up enough to help them. They decided, therefore, to launch a public relations and fundraising campaign for the Statue's refurbishing.

But even that did not seem to be measuring up. An internal communication memorandum to the director notes, "Only 'small fry' from the newly-formed United Nations had visited the Statue. So far as we can ascertain, none of the big names have been here."

There was one bright spot, however. The same memorandum goes on to note, "Norman Rockwell, the famous artist, visited the Statue on March 19 to gather data which he is using for the preparation of the July 4 cover of The Saturday Evening Post. It is planned to have the torch shown with men performing maintenance work on it, to symbolize the light of Liberty being kept burning. Mr. Rockwell indicated that this symbolism would bring in the United Nations but it was not entirely clear to us how he is doing this."

ᔕ

In early March, 1946, Norman Rockwell traveled from his home in West Arlington, Vermont to New York City for a meeting with *Saturday Evening Post* art editor Ken Stuart. The purpose of the meeting was to flesh out a concept for the July 4th cover.

Agreement had been reached on portraying the Statue of Liberty. Both men wanted the cover to depict the patriotism of the American citizens, yet without any blatant "flag-waving."

Since there was a campaign afoot to raise money for the refurbishment of the Statue and its grounds, Rockwell wondered whether that might somehow be portrayed. An illustration of Liberty being maintained to keep her clean and strong could be a powerful symbol.

But Rockwell never painted anything that had not, or was not, actually happening. Did the Statue of Liberty ever really get cleaned?

Stuart and Rockwell got on the phone to Mr. Marshall, the then-custodian of the Statue of Liberty. Marshall confirmed that, although the entire statue was never cleaned, the torch was cleaned annually. Every July, steeplejacks scaled the arm (which begins 300 feet from the ground) to clean the heavy amber glass of the torch. The authenticity of Rockwell's cover idea was established.

Rockwell now needed photos. Since the workmen would not be there until July, and the cover was due to appear that same month, he would have to take pictures of the torch without the workmen and figure out the rest later.

The illustrator was prepared to hire a plane to get an overhead view of the Statue. But Rockwell found that a perfect angle for the photographer's shots could be achieved from the top of the monument's administration building.

Upon returning home to West Arlington, Rockwell persuaded a man from the area named Sousy, a former steeplejack, to model for the workmen figures. The artist propped a ladder against his barn, then Sousy climbed it and struck various poses while holding a paint brush and a bucket.

The composite result of both the Statue and the Sousy photos is captured in four sketches, sketches which reveal the stages Rockwell and his editor Ken Stuart went through as they conceptualized the illustration.

Sketch one, drawn by Rockwell, shows Lady Liberty's outstretched arm holding the torch aloft against the backdrop of the Manhattan skyline. In this first sketch, only three men are at work cleaning the lamp.

In sketch two, drawn by Stuart, the head and crown of the statue are included, and the statue is viewed from the rear. Of these changes, Rockwell notes, "That's what I call creative art editing." It is also in sketch two that Stuart substitutes a Rockwell look-alike for one of the three workmen. There is no record of Rockwell commenting on this whimsical bit of editing.

The third sketch, done by Rockwell with watercolors rather than charcoal, was intended to portray the Statue surrounded with a stormy sky, symbolizing the troubled times of World War II. But neither Rockwell nor Stuart thought much of that drawing.

In the fourth and final sketch, Rockwell went back to charcoal. He added two more workmen, including one hanging a bucket off the rim of the torch itself. The artist wished to emphasize the 42-foot-long length of the Statue's arm.

In this last sketch, the one from which the painting for the *Post* cover would be created, Rockwell also lightened the sky and darkened the features of the workman furthest to the right, the one in the red shirt. No records indicate whether or not Ken Stuart signed off on this final draft.

Was this done with complicity or duplicity? We may never know. But however he did it, Norman Rockwell got a brown man into "Working on

The Statue of Liberty" and onto the cover of *The Saturday Evening Post.* Hopefully the patriotic painting would boost not only the spirits of the American people, but the fortunes of the Statue of Liberty monument refurbishing fund as well. It didn't.

ꟹ

The report to the director of the monument for July, 1946 indicated that the Statue of Liberty was still in trouble. The document carried a decidedly peevish tone. The weather had remained hot and dry, ideal conditions for visitors but "bad effect on our lawns". When rain finally did arrive at the end of the month, only "such grass as had not been killed by visitors and newspaper men began to recover".

Journalists were apparently not regarded as assets. The report complained of "reporters and photographers who invariably managed to arrive at inconvenient times".

This dissatisfaction carried over to the report-writers' assessment of Norman Rockwell's July 4th cover: they didn't like it. "From the people with whom we have talked it seems that Rockwell's idea of the symbolism of the torch completely failed to go across".

ꟹ

Norman Rockwell's painting "Working on the Statue of Liberty" was donated to the White House in 1994 by Steven Spielberg, a devoted Rockwell collector. It now hangs in the Oval Office, right behind the President's desk chair.

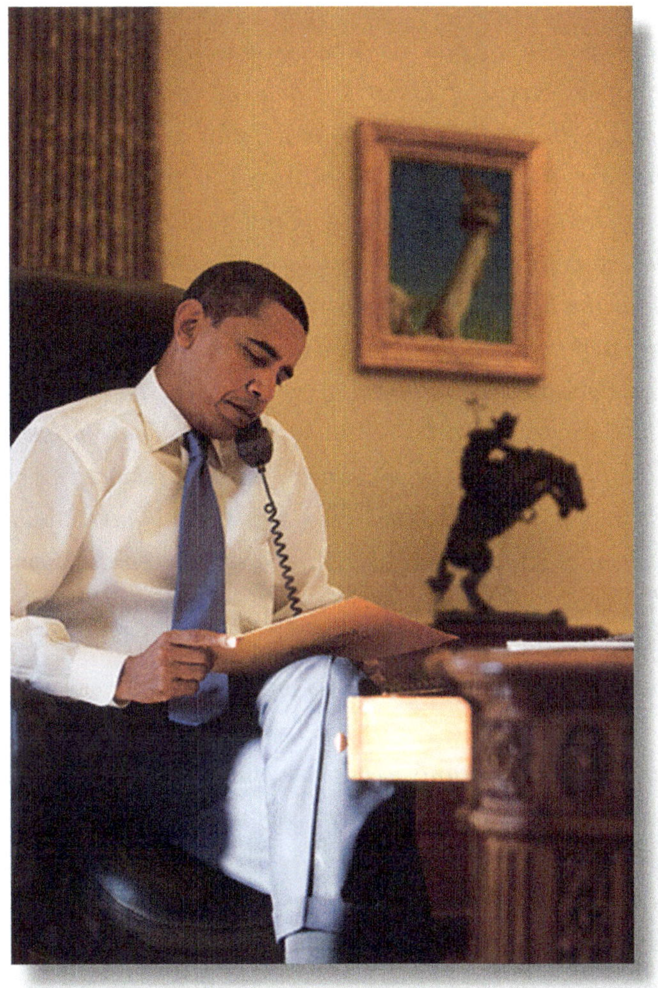

President Barack Obama in Oval Office, January 21, 2009

While minutely scouring Norman Rockwell Post covers for depictions of people of color, I was startled to unexpectedly find one in "Working on The Statue of Liberty." Hanging off the right side of Liberty's torch, the workman in the red shirt appeared to be brown.

At first I couldn't believe my eyes. But after enlarging a reproduction of the cover to a gazillion times its size, and then having trusted associates do a cross-check on my eyesight and sanity, the verdict remained the same: that man is brown.

I have been able to find no other commentary or popular reaction to "Working on The Statue of Liberty." I have no idea what people the report writers talked with or why the symbolism "failed to go across." But I cannot help but wonder: did some of "the powers that be" notice Rockwell's diversity statement and take offense? Did they think this was Rockwell's way of "bringing in the United Nations"? "Whatever the case, "Working on the Statue of Liberty," and the brown workman in it, dropped from the radar, including from the sights of noted Rockwell historians. To date, the brown workman and the Norman Rockwell look-alike on top of Lady Liberty's torch continue to be hidden in plain sight, right above President Obama's chair in the Oval Office.

At least I think they are. On November 15, 2011, I showed my enlargements of the Statue of Liberty illustration to Stephanie Plunkett, Chief Curator for the Norman Rockwell Museum. After a brief stunned silence, Plunkett whispered, "He was not supposed to be there," referring to the brown workman hanging off of the side of the torch, as well as to the Norman Rockwell look-alike. Apparently, up until this point, no one had noticed or documented their presence in the painting.

Appearing on the museum's website on January 4, 2010, for example, is a description of the July 4, 1946 Saturday Evening Post *cover as "repair workers (miniscule by comparison) doing their best to keep the symbolic torch alive". No mention was made of the brown worker or the Rockwell look-alike.*

Plunkett and I agreed that the original painting, now hanging in the Oval Office, needed to be inspected to verify the pigmentation of the worker and the presence of the Rockwell look-alike. She offered to ask William G. Allman, Chief of the White House Office of The Curator and a friend of the Norman Rockwell Museum, to inspect the painting and give us a verdict. Plunkett promised to get back to me. I waited to hear from her.

After four weeks of silence and of getting no response to either my phone or email follow-ups, I decided to take another tack. Counting on the power of the press, I shared my "scoop" with Randy Kennedy, visual arts writer and critic for The New York Times.

Kennedy attempted to talk with the White House but, as he perplexedly informed me by email on February 27, 2012, "I've had no luck getting William Allman at the White House to respond. . . ", even though the Times *reporter and Allman had a close professional relationship and had worked together on other stories in the past.*

Kennedy went on to say that, after several tries, he had finally spoken with Stephanie Plunkett at the Norman Rockwell Museum. According to Kennedy, Plunkett now theorized that "the brown worker may have drawn no notice because, given that the figure in the painting was a worker, it somehow didn't contravene the Post's *policy of presenting African-Americans only in subservient roles and didn't ruffle any feathers with the* Post's *leadership at the time." The museum had not contacted the White House curator, William Allman, regarding the matter.*

The Times *art critic continued: "It's hard to know. And without anything from the historical record, it's hard for me know what the story is here. If this were indeed a discovery it would certainly be a story. But it seems to me that viewers of the* Post *cover and of the painting over the years had to be aware that the worker wasn't white - it's just too clear. As to why there seems to have been no commentary about the fact, that's something I'm now trying to figure out."*

As of this writing, this is a question we're all still trying to figure out. And as far as I know, the brown workman in "Working on The Statue of Liberty" remains undocumented.

Hidden in Plain Sight

Randy Kennedy's comments succinctly capture the enigma surrounding people of color in Norman Rockwell's work. The brown workman on top of Rockwell's Statue of Liberty is so clear that people have been looking right through him for over sixty years. And there's been no commentary about him because nobody expects him to be there.

Until I began my research, nobody went looking for colored people in Norman Rockwell paintings. To Rockwell's annoyance throughout his life and to my confused amazement to this day, the world has just kept on believing that Norman Rockwell's America, just like Norman Rockwell's neighborhoods and Norman Rockwell's Statue of Liberty, is all white.

Chapter 3

THE ROCKWELL MODELS OF WASHINGTON COUNTY

"Most of the time I try to entertain with my Post *covers. But once in a while I get the uncontrollable urge to say something serious."*
Norman Rockwell

Norman Rockwell loved Franklin Delano Roosevelt. And he was ecstatic about Roosevelt's New Deal. As FDR's progressive programs started to roll out, Rockwell enthusiastically submitted two covers glorifying the reforms to the *Saturday Evening Post.*

But George Horace Lorimer, editor-in-chief of the popular magazine, was in no mood to "get liberal." He rejected both Rockwell submissions and had them completely destroyed. No record exists of what they looked like. Stung by such fierce rejection, Norman Rockwell pulled even deeper into his persona as "avatar of the New England homestead."

However, in 1951, as Niemeyer and Le Corbusier's glorious building soared upwards towards completion on the bank of the East River, the illustrator again began thinking about "saying something serious": a tribute to the newly-formed United Nations. Rockwell envisioned a large mural displaying all of the peoples of the world amassed behind the dais of the United Nations Security Council delegates.

But as the concept became clearer, a problem inherently connected with it became clearer, as well. Vermont was virtually all white. Most of the peoples of the world were not. Where was Norman Rockwell going to find colored models? The answer was across the state line in Washington County, New York.

A Brief History of Washington County

Washington County, New York is part of that labyrinth of valleys and watersheds which begins south at New York City (where the Hudson River empties into the Atlantic) and ends north at the Canadian border (where the Saint Lawrence River flows into Lake Champlain). The towns of Washington County are at a mid-point in this system, and because of this, they achieved immediate and enormous financial success with the building of the Champlain Canal in 1823. The canal runs right across the county, providing a direct water connection between the Hudson River and the southern end of Lake Champlain. The creation of the Champlain Canal also established a section of the Underground Railroad that came to be known as "The Champlain Line."

The Champlain Line ran up the Hudson River, through the Champlain Canal and on into Lake Champlain and Canada. Tens of thousands of self-emancipated black folks made their way to freedom along this route. The old Coach Road (New York State Route 40), part of the railroad, ran parallel to the Champlain Canal through secluded farm country, straight to the town of Greenwich, New York.

Greenwich, with its several Quaker-owned safe houses, was a critical station on the Champlain Line. Ever since the Quakers migrated there from Rhode Island in 1790, they found themselves in open battle with the established Puritan citizens over the question of slavery. However, in 1827, slavery was abolished throughout the state of New York. Immediately, Greenwich's Quaker culture took pre-eminence and the town became a center of the national abolitionist movement.

Local doctor Hiram Corliss and eleven other prominent Greenwich citizens left the Dutch Reformed Church and founded their own assembly, the Congregational Church, specifically so they could preach and teach the principles of abolitionism. The Congregational Church hosted such well-known anti-slavery lecturers as Frederick Douglass and Horace Greeley. Hiram Corliss' home, situated along the Battenkill River at 12 Bridge Street, was one of the stations on the Underground Railroad.

Local free black families also provided shelter to runaway slaves. By 1850, more than a dozen African-American families resided in Greenwich,

New York. Other unmarried individuals of color worked as cooks, barbers or servants in nearby hotels.

During this same period, Greenwich became home to noted abolitionist and suffragette Susan B. Anthony. Anthony's Quaker family had moved to the community in 1826 when she was six years old. Nearly forty years later, another illustrious resident arrived in Greenwich: Grandma Moses.

Grandma Moses, Norman Rockwell, and The Adams Family of Washington County

Born Anna Mary Robertson, Grandma Moses was born and spent her youth in Greenwich, New York. In 1887, at the age of 27, she married Thomas Salmon Moses and moved to Virginia where she raised five children before returning to Washington County in 1907.

In 1938, Anna Moses primitive folk paintings were "discovered" by New York City art collector Louis J. Caldor. He spotted the artist's work in the window of a local drug store, drove to Moses' farm home in Eagle Bridge, New York that very same afternoon, and bought all of her paintings.

Within a year, Moses' work was on display at the *New York Museum of Modern Art*. A private show at a New York gallery was a critical and financial smash hit. Washington County resident "Grandma Moses" soared to celebrity status.

❧

When the Norman Rockwell family moved to Arlington in 1938, they were just across the state line and down the Battenkill River from Grandma Moses' home. The two famous artists became close friends. For example in September, 1948, the Rockwells hosted an 88th-birthday celebration for Moses at their Arlington home. That same year, Grandma Moses appeared as part of the welcoming party in Norman Rockwell's December 25th *Saturday Evening Post* cover, "Christmas Homecoming."

❧

As a native of the area, Grandma Moses had many friends among the other old families of Washington County, both black and white. One of these friends was Martha May Driggiss.

Martha May Driggiss was the second youngest of seven children born to Morris Driggiss and Belle Newcomb. Morris, a mixed-race man of Susquehanna Indian and black descent, had migrated from the state of Delaware to the town of Cambridge in Washington County. There he established an 88-acre homestead at the top of a rise locally referred to as "Cobble Mound." Belle Newcomb, his wife, was the mulatto daughter of a local white doctor and a black mother whose family had been part of the free black community in Washington County since the early 1800's.

Their daughter, Martha May, was a striking woman with golden skin, flowing black hair and hazel eyes. Beautiful but somewhat haughty, she had little time for local suitors. But when Major Libby Adams, a black man fifteen years her junior, appeared in town, Martha May was swept off of her feet.

ꕥ

Major Adams was a native of the historic Bahamian community in Key West, Florida. A beating he had received attempting to defend his sister against the unwelcome advances of several white men had left him with a metal plate in his head and a need to quickly escape Florida.

About the same time as this tragic incident, Dave Moore, owner of an automobile repair shop in Cambridge, New York, placed an ad in a Key West newspaper. He was looking for a mechanic's apprentice, someone wanting to come North and willing to work (to begin with, at least) for transportation, room and board. Major Adams applied.

Dave Moore, epitomizing Washington County's Underground Railroad heritage, gave the beleaguered black man the job. When Moore met his new apprentice at the train station, the man was still wearing the beach sandals of the Keys.

Major Adams spotted Martha May Driggiss on the streets of Cambridge almost immediately. They married within months of meeting. The couple's first child, Carl, was born in 1942, followed by Paul in 1945, Pauline in 1947 and Mary Beth in 1950.

Adams was, however, an erratic provider. His head injuries and resultant surgeries contributed to his unpredictable, often violent behavior. When, in 1952, Adams finally deserted the family completely, the entire Cambridge community, including his wife, breathed a collective sigh of relief. But Martha May, a fifth-generation Washington County native, now found herself alone with four children, all under the age of twelve, and no immediate means of support.

The community moved swiftly to aid the destitute mother. Martha May found a part-time position as a dietary aid at Mary McClelland Hospital. She worked as a nanny for wealthy families in the area. And she assembled her young brood into a gospel singing group and took them on the road.

Often, after Major deserted the family, they had gathered in the evenings to sing hymns. There was no car in which to take excursions, and their television only received one channel.

Martha May would guide the children through songs in intricate three-, sometimes four-part harmonies. Washington County neighbors, white and black, started coming to her home to hear the little group sing. One of these neighbors was Grandma Moses.

Moses had been a close friend of Belle Driggiss, Martha May's mother. The folk artist had known Martha since she was a child. Enchanted by the gospel singing group, Grandma Moses invited Martha to bring the children up to her home to perform. Several other influential residents of Washington County were in attendance, as well. All were enthralled. A "good will" offering was taken and given to Martha May. Arrangements were made for future performances in other venues. "The Adams Children Gospel Singing Group" was launched.

The little quartet became something of a local sensation, performing in numerous churches and private homes throughout the region. Audiences delighted in hearing the children deliver their renditions of "Do Lord, Oh Do Lord, Oh Do Remember Me" and "It Is No Secret What God Can Do." Everyone in Washington County knew the Adams children.

So when Norman Rockwell confided to his friend Grandma Moses that he was having trouble finding models for "the peoples of the world" he wanted to include in a mural he was crafting for the United Nations, Moses immediately recommended her friend Martha May Adams and "The Adams Children Gospel Singing Group."

The Adams Family Models for Norman Rockwell's UN Mural

On a crisp winter morning in 1952, Cambridge, New York's only taxi cab pulled up in front of the modest frame house at 495 Cobble Road. The cab's driver and owner, Bill Butler, got out to help Carl, Paul, Pauline and Mary Beth Adams into the back seat of the cab. Then he assisted their mother, Martha May Adams, as she seated herself in the front.

The Adams family could not afford a car. Usually when they had a singing engagement, their transport was the program's organizers. But this outing was no routine singing engagement. This appointment was different. Butler had been hired to chauffeur the little group twenty minutes up Route 313 (now Route 7A), then across the Battenkill River to West Arlington, Vermont–to the studio of the internationally famous artist, Norman Rockwell.

ɞ

Pauline Adams Grimes was only five years old on that special occasion. But sixty years later, she remembers it as if it were yesterday.

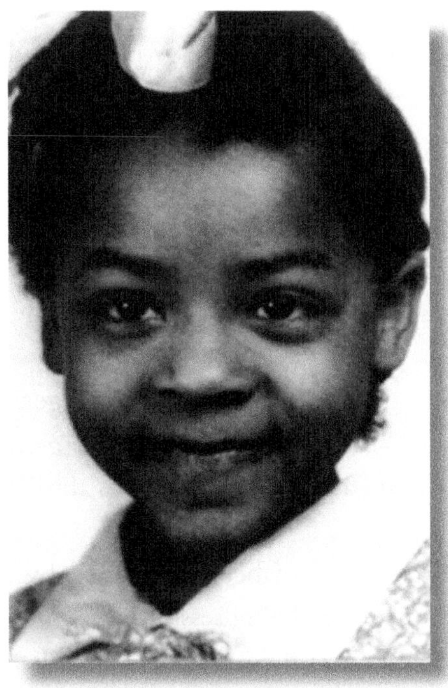

Pauline Adams at Five Years Old

"Mother fussed all week before our expedition to Arlington," Grimes recalls, "mending, washing and ironing our 'Sunday best'. " The boys, Carl and Paul, were especially turned out: starched, buttoned up shirts and dress trousers sporting razor sharp creases pressed into each leg.

When Butler's taxi pulled up in front of Norman Rockwell's snowbound studio, the quiet excitement pulsating from the brood in the back seat burst into open amazement. It was all just too much: getting off from school, being all dressed up in the middle of the week, a cab ride to another state, and now this. The children's eyes grew wide as saucers: there, sticking out of the sundrenched snow drifts, twinkling like amber jewels, were bottles and bottles of Coca Cola!

In 1952, a bottle of Coca Cola was a big deal. For poor children such as the Adams clan, the sight of piles of this treat chilling in the snow was a vision beyond belief.

As they tumbled out of the taxi, Martha May sternly admonished her offspring not to even think about touching one of those bottles. Then the studio door opened and the entire group, including the cab's driver Bill Butler, was ushered inside by none other than Mr. and Mrs. Norman Rockwell.

Mary Rockwell helped the children out of their winter wraps while Norman stooped down to greet each tyke individually, handing each of them their very own bottle of Coke. For little three-year-old Mary Beth, the bottle was almost as big as she was. But, like the others, she happily imbibed.

"I was a shy child, usually very afraid of strangers," her sister, Pauline Adams Grimes recalls. "But Mr. Rockwell was so gentle and kind to us. I was not nervous with him at all. None of us was afraid with him as we were with others."

After sodas and cookies had been consumed by all, Rockwell began bringing out props for the modeling session. Then he stared at seven-year-old Paul Adams. "Please take off your shirt," the illustrator asked the boy.

Hesitating only a moment, Paul reached up to his neck and proceeded to unbutton the carefully laundered and ironed shirt his mother had prepared for him. Handing the garment to his surprised and somewhat bewildered mother, Paul, now in his undershirt, turned again to face the artist.

"Your undershirt too, please?" Rockwell asked. At this, Paul's alarmed mother uttered a sharp cry. What was going on here?

The illustrator, deep into his own conceptualizing, realized he had explained nothing to Martha May Adams. "I want him to be a little African boy," Rockwell enlightened the now clearly agitated mom. He then explained his idea for a United Nations mural depicting the peoples of the world. A relieved Martha May smiled a sigh of relief, took the undershirt from her youngest son's hands, and sat down.

Photos of this studio session show that Carl lost his Sunday best shirt as well for the sake of Rockwellian authenticity. Five-year-old Pauline Adams wears only her sleeveless white ruffled slip, bare arms at her sides, tiny fingers encircling a covered urn held in front of her.

Although Rockwell did not ask Martha May to disrobe, he did have her braid her hair into two shining plaits, hanging over her shoulders. Then, sheathed in what appears to be a multicolored blanket, arms crossed over her bodice, the regal woman assumed a pose more reflective of her Native American ancestors than her African ones.

Only little Mary May seems to have escaped a Rockwell makeover. In the archival photos she is seen staring back at the camera, thumb in mouth, her white puff-sleeved dress with matching socks and shoes sparkling clean, not a spilled drop of Coca Cola to be seen anywhere.

The Adams family photo shoot at Norman Rockwell's Arlington studio took about three hours. Pictures were taken of them both individually and in groups. The artist gently yet firmly coaxed each model into various expressions and poses, often acting them out himself, to the great delight of the usually reticent Adams children.

At the end of the session, Bill Butler, awed that he had gotten to spend an afternoon watching Norman Rockwell at work, was further delighted when the famous illustrator paid the cabbie for his waiting time as well as for the trips from Cambridge and back. Rockwell also paid Martha May Adams fifteen dollars for each of the five models including little Mary May, which was five dollars more than what he usually paid his models. No doubt the artist was aware that the struggling single mother could use some extra cash.

As the group bundled up to leave, Pauline Adams Grimes clearly remembers Norman Rockwell pointing to the remaining sodas still glistening just outside his studio door. "Help yourselves on the way out," he offered. But whether she didn't hear him or she didn't wish to hear him, Pauline's mother ignored the invitation of her celebrity host.

Glaring "no!" at her offspring as they reached longingly for the snowbound delicacies, a dignified Martha May Driggiss Adams guided her little troupe of gospel singers (now little Norman Rockwell models, as well) back towards Bill Butler's taxi and home, home to Washington County.

The Fate of Rockwell's United Nations Mural (and The Adams Family Models Who Posed For It)

In his autobiography, Norman Rockwell exclaims, "Every so often I get to hankering after immortality and, or so I think at those times anyway, that requires a picture tremendously conceived and tremendously executed."

Rockwell intended to create a United Nations painting that would be both. To his way of thinking, the UN was the only way to help the world "out of the mess it's in." But trying to execute the concept turned out to be an even bigger mess.

Rockwell's vision was a mural depicting members of the United Nations Security Council sitting at a dais looking out at the viewer. Behind the delegates in the shadows would be "the people of the world," sixty-five persons in all, "waiting for the delegates to straighten out the world so that they might live in peace and without fear."

The public relations department of the UN gave the illustrator permission to take photos inside the building, and to actually photograph the delegates in the Security Council chamber.

When Norman Rockwell began making trips down to the United Nations for the photo shoots, the delegates to the Security Council were the USSR, the United States, the United Kingdom and Chile–the country holding the rotating seat on the Council.

Norman Rockwell's first photo session was with Henry Cabot Lodge, United States ambassador to the United Nations. Ambassador Lodge sat and stared into the camera.

"Would you smile, Mr. Lodge?" the artist asked. "No," snapped Lodge. "I can't do that. You take it like this." The British, then the Chilean delegate, each followed the same suit: neither could or would act. Both looked unhappy.

The last photo session was with Andrei Vishinsky, the Russian ambassador to the UN and a Security Council member. He had demanded to see a preliminary sketch of the mural to assure it contained no caricatures or derogatory portrayals of the Russian people. So Mary Rockwell traveled down to meet with Vishinsky, show him the drafts and gain his approval. Their meeting was an overwhelming success: not only did Vishinsky (through a translator) voice enthusiastic approval for the mural, he also voiced enthusiastic approval for Mary Rockwell, as well.

The Russian Ambassador, ready for his photo shoot with Norman Rockwell, entered the Security Council chamber flanked by two bodyguards dressed in black, their hands plunged into their pockets. Through an interpreter, Rockwell asked the ambassador to take a seat. Andrei Vishinsky was all smiles.

This, however, was not a good thing. Since the previous three delegates had *not* smiled, the artist couldn't depict the Russian this way: it would look like "Santa Claus strayed into a den of Scrooges." Again through the interpreter, Rockwell asked Vishinsky not to smile but "just to look pleasant."

Back at his studio in Vermont, Rockwell spent the next four weeks photographing and sketching over thirty models, including the Adams family. Selected sketches were arranged to create a composite of figures of various nationalities comprising the "peoples of the world". I have not yet been able to identify all of the models of color in this composite, but two are clearly recognizable. On the far right and bottom, the little black girl with her hands folded in prayer is Pauline Adams. And front and center, standing between the seated United Kingdom and United States ambassadors, is her brother, Paul Adams.

Norman Rockwell spent another month on a preliminary rendering of the mural in charcoal. Then, just as the illustrator completed the 10' x 10' panel, Vishinsky was recalled to Moscow and a new Russian delegate was assigned to the Security Council. So Rockwell had to go back to the United Nations and take new photographs.

This time, however, when he returned to Vermont, the artist did not dive back into working on the mural. Instead, Rockwell propped the panel on a spare easel in his studio and turned to catch up on his regular work, work neglected over the past two months.

Weeks passed, and as Rockwell looked at the delegates and the "peoples" behind them, he began to have doubts about the whole concept. As he says in his autobiography, "I turned the charcoal to the wall. I couldn't stand to look at it any more. It seemed empty and pretentious. Then I rolled it up and stored it away in the back room."

That was the end of The Big Picture. And that was the end of the Adams family's posing as Rockwell models. At least for a while.

ℰ

Forty-eight years later, on a cool September morning in 2010, Pauline Adams Grimes and I met for breakfast. Pauline suggested we dine at the appropriately-named Country Gals Cafe, located on Main Street in Cambridge, New York (Washington, County) just a few doors from the once famous, now somewhat infamous, Cambridge Hotel.

Established in 1885, the hotel's greatest claim to fame was as the home of pie a la mode. Changing vacation tastes coupled with poor management over the years finally led to the closing of the Cambridge Hotel in June, 2012. However, this was not before the historic hostelry was visited by celebrity chef Gordon Ramsay for an episode of his reality show, "Hotel Hell." The difference between the before and after was spectacular, but not enough to keep the doors open.

As Pauline and I walked through the kitchen of the Country Gals Cafe, moving from the jammed front to the quieter back room, young employees of the local breakfast emporium were peeling potatoes and rapidly replenishing the mounds of home fries sizzling on the grill. Looking over at Pauline as we seated ourselves at a Formica table, I recognized the brown porcelain doll-like glowing cheeks and sparkling eyes of the little girl Norman Rockwell eventually showcased, first in his famous Saturday Evening Post *cover, "The Golden Rule," and then in his illustration for the* Look Magazine *article, "How Goes The War on Poverty."*

Pauline Grimes, married to a retired high school principal and grandmother of four, has resided in Cambridge all of her life: "sixth generation" she will quickly, but pleasantly, tell you. Moreover, Grimes still owns 40 of the 88 original acres homesteaded by her grandfather Morris Driggiss atop Cobble Mount. The house she, her mother and her siblings were living in the second time Norman Rockwell sought them out as models is still there. After breakfast, we took a ride to see it.

Traveling west out of town, on Main Street going towards Greenwich, we turned left onto Route 59, then right onto Cobble Road about two miles farther along. A third of the way up the mount, a simple, single-story house sat off the south side of the road across from the rising hill face. In this modest dwelling, on a sunny day in 1954, Pauline's mother, Martha May Driggiss Adams, was able to return Mr. Rockwell's hospitality.

The Adams Family Are Rockwell Models, Again

Norman Rockwell had telephoned Mrs. Adams earlier in the week, asking if he and his photographer could come up and take more photographs of the children. By this time, Rockwell had left Arlington and moved to Stockbridge, Massachusetts, so it was easier for him to come to the family than for the family to come to him.

Not surprisingly, Martha May enthusiastically said "yes." Again, several days of intense mending, washing and ironing ensued. When Norman Rockwell knocked at the front door, Carl, Paul, Pauline and Mary Beth Adams were all clean and pressed and waiting, ready to model again.

As the artist renewed his acquaintance with each of the Adams children, their mother quietly went into the kitchen, picked up a galvanized pail, and slipped out the door to the backyard pump. A few minutes later, just as Rockwell and his photographer were starting to set up the lighting for the photos, Martha May Driggiss Adams came into the living room with two glasses of water and two folded paper napkins on a tray. She could not afford Coca Cola. But Cobble Mount had the sweetest water in all of Cambridge.

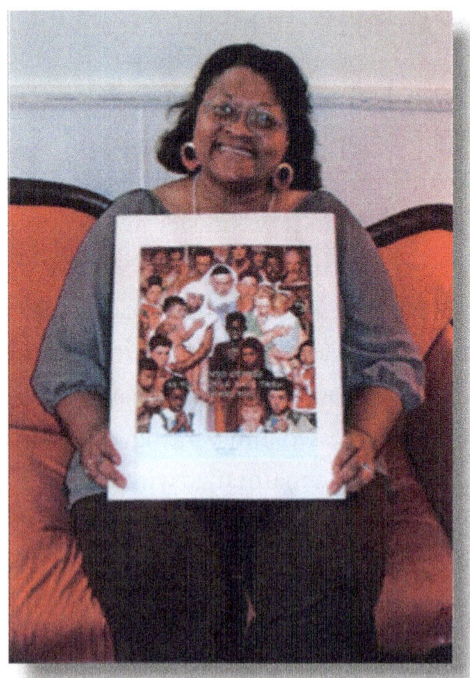

Pauline Adams Grimes Holding a Copy of The Golden Rule

Norman Rockwell took photos of all four of the children that day. He focused particularly, however, on face shots of Pauline and of her older brother, Paul. It is Paul who captures the gaze front and center in "The Golden Rule" appearing, like his sister, with all the beauty, mystery and intensity of a brown porcelain doll. It is, in fact, around the matter of dolls that Rockwell model Pauline Adams Grimes story turns somewhat sad. Pauline made the mistake of thinking that she might have the right to benefit from being a Norman Rockwell model.

The World of Norman Rockwell Collectibles, Especially The Dolls

Norman Rockwell collectibles are a widespread and somewhat peculiar phenomenon across the American landscape. For decades, folks across the country have salted away ashtrays, coffee cups, tea cozies, Christmas ornaments, key chains and all other sorts of bric-a-brac with reproductions of Rockwell illustrations on them, many in the hope that someday these "collections" will be worth as much as the original Norman Rockwell paintings themselves.

The person most likely responsible for launching this craze into high gear is probably a woman named Mary Moline. In 1978, the year Rockwell died, Moline composed the "Norman Rockwell Encyclopedia" for the Curtis Publishing Company (owners of *The Saturday Evening Post*). Since the artist had passed away in November and the Encyclopedia came out that very same year, I think it is safe to say that the book was put together rather quickly. Although it is the first chronological catalogue of Norman Rockwell's work, the substance of the compendium fell somewhat short of being encyclopedic: it is now out of print.

That same year, however, Mary Moline also published (through her own outlet, Rumbleseat Press) a "Norman Rockwell Collectibles Value Guide: The Little Rockwell Book." The book purported to list "everything Rockwell," giving the original cost of each collectible, setting values, listing manufacturers, titles, the number and date of items made, and, (did I already mention this?) setting values.

The "Value Guide" had seven editions. Its first was one hundred-fifty pages long. Ten years later in 1988, when the sixth edition appeared, the "Norman Rockwell Collectibles Value Guide" had grown to 284 pages, and included 1500 photographs. The value of the "Value Guide" seemed to be doing quite well.

The last edition of Mary Moline's book appeared in 2002, and it was around this time that Pauline Adams Grimes began to explore the idea of creating some Norman Rockwell collectibles of her own. According to the "Guide," Norman Rockwell Character Dolls, dolls in the likenesses of subjects portrayed in Rockwell paintings, commanded top dollar in the collectibles world. Excited at the prospect of establishing another income stream for her family, Grimes considered creating a set of "Paul and Pauline" dolls, figures modeled after her and her brother in Rockwell's famous painting, "The Golden Rule." She envisioned commanding a few of those collectors' top dollars for herself.

But what Pauline Adams Grimes did not know was that Mary Moline, the valuator of the Norman Rockwell Character Dolls, had also been the *manufacturer* of the Norman Rockwell Character Dolls and, in the end, that venture had not gone well for her at all.

ᔓ

A year after Norman Rockwell's death, in 1979, Mary Moline signed a three-year licensing agreement with Curtis Publishing Company. The agreement allowed her to produce twenty different Norman Rockwell character dolls, with 20,000 copies made of each one. Manufactured in West Germany, the 10"-tall porcelain dolls were to be hand painted and numbered, each with its own identification imprinted on the back of its neck.

The character doll series began with the "Mimi" doll, a little girl in a green coat and red beret. There followed an "Anne" doll, a "Nell" doll, a "Sally" doll. There was even a "Little Girl and Her Doll" doll. The plan was that the twentieth and last item in the series would be a "Norman Rockwell" doll, accompanied by a miniature *Saturday Evening Post* paperboy.

In 1981, the third year of Moline's contract with Curtis, the "Wilma" doll appeared. Her cocoa brown skin, thick black plaits and sparkling white dress proclaimed that this doll was the little black girl in Norman Rockwell's iconic illustration, "The Problem We All Live With." The "Wilma" doll flew out of the West Germany factory doors. And almost immediately, its "value," and that of the entire Rockwell doll series, really took off.

By 1985, the entire Norman Rockwell Character Doll collection was at the height of its popularity. For example, that year the theme of the Greene County (Pennsylvania) Historical Society's fifth annual dollhouse exhibit was "The Norman Rockwell Era," with special tribute paid to doll creator Mary Moline. Moline, in fact, graciously donated several dolls to the Society as prizes for the exhibition's fund-raising raffle.

Much of this public relations activity, however, may have been to camouflage the legal tug-of-war that was going on over the dolls between Mary Moline and Curtis Publishing. Since 1983, Moline had been producing the dolls without a license from Curtis. The company had notified Moline that it was not renewing its permission for her to produce the dolls, stating that it was contracting with another party to make them. Curtis wanted to make a less expensive version of the line. Mary Moline countered through her lawyers, however, that Curtis had no right to terminate their agreement, and kept on shipping the little Norman Rockwell character lookalikes out of her West German workshops.

Then, in January of 1985, Curtis Publishing asked a federal court to make Moline stop producing the dolls. Instead, the judge referred the matter to binding arbitration. While the arbitrators considered the case, Mary Moline kept turning out dolls and reporting their values in updated editions of "The Value Guide."

Finally, in 1989, the court-appointed arbitration board made its determination: Curtis Publishing had been within its rights when it declined to renew a contract with Mary Moline. Moline was fined $200,000 for failure to stop making dolls after her three-year license had ended. She was also ordered to cease and desist from any further manufacture of Norman Rockwell Character Dolls. If there were any Rockwell dolls to be made, Curtis Publishing was going to be the one making them.

Pauline Adams Grimes knew of none of this as she dreamed of creating a tidy nest egg for herself and her family by producing a line of "Paul and Pauline" Norman Rockwell dolls. She did her research and found "Donna's Children", a custom doll manufacturer right across the state line in Springfield, Massachusetts.

"Donna's Children," a custom doll design and manufacturing business is owned and operated by its founder, Donna Sabonis. In 2005, Pauline Grimes contacted Sabonis and discussed with her the concept of producing "Paul and Pauline" dolls. The doll maker shared Pauline's enthusiasm for the idea. "Donna's Children" had the capacity to design the molds as well as produce, package and distribute the dolls. Pauline, being the actual Rockwell model, would be a natural for marketing and sales. The two women agreed to collaborate.

Pauline had seen the financial potential of being a Norman Rockwell model close up, although she had not benefited much from it herself. The Norman Rockwell Museum in Arlington, Vermont (now closed), a combination of art gallery and gift shop, frequently asked Pauline and her brother Paul to come over from Cambridge to share with gallery visitors their remembrances and experiences as Rockwell models, and to autograph illustration reprints and other Rockwell paraphernalia on sale at the shop. The models were allowed to receive tips for their autographs, but that was their only remuneration. After a while, Paul Adams refused to be involved in any activity relating to Norman Rockwell.

Pauline, however, continued to volunteer at the museum. It was on one of these occasions, while chatting with visitors about her plans for the "Paul and Pauline" dolls that she learned of Curtis Publishing and the fly she then feared might be in her ointment. Curtis Publishing, it seemed, owned the rights to any image that appeared on a *Saturday Evening Post* cover–even if it was an image of oneself.

Pauline Adams Grimes immediately got in touch with the giant publishing house at their corporate offices in Indianapolis, Indiana. Surely, she thought, she should be able to make a doll of herself.

Encountering the Publisher Who Doesn't Publish

"Now is the perfect time to consider licensing art work from the *Saturday Evening Post* in your production line, corporate communications, advertising/promotion campaigns or media productions." Thus cheerily proclaims the website of The Curtis Publishing Company, a company which ironically, since 1968, no longer publishes anything. Curtis Publishing's sole activity is the sale of licenses.

In response to Pauline Grimes' inquiry, Curtis Publishing informed her that: 1) she could not produce any representation of herself as she appeared in any *Saturday Evening Post* issue without the express permission and license of Curtis Publishing Company and 2) permission to use her "Golden Rule" image in a doll would cost $1000 startup and a percentage of each doll made. Pauline Adams Grimes did not have $1000.

Grimes attempted to negotiate with Curtis, asking them to let her start production and pay them back when profits started coming in. But it was no deal. She put the prototypes of "Paul and Pauline" in the back of a closet in her Cambridge home, and let that dream fade away.

☙

As Pauline and I put together the pieces of her story, it became hauntingly clear to me that something was seriously out of whack. The same little girl to whom Norman Rockwell, had handed modeling fees and as much Coca Cola as she could drink (to help him create iconic statements about the brotherhood of man), now needed to pay a corporate entity in Indiana for the right to reproduce her own image.

Chapter 4

MOVING ON: THE LITTLE BLACK GIRL(S) IN THE LITTLE WHITE DRESS

"For 47 years, I portrayed the best of all possible worlds–grandfathers, puppy dogs–things like that. That kind of stuff is dead now, and I think it's about time."
Norman Rockwell

Leaving the Doll House

Norman Rockwell's white clapboard farmhouse on the shores of the Battenkill River in Vermont may have looked like a doll house. But for Mary Rockwell, the artist's second wife and mother to his three sons, life was more Ibsen-like than idyllic. Similar to the protagonist in Henrik Ibsen's play, "The Doll House," Mary Rockwell felt disillusioned and abandoned–abandoned, in this case, by her workaholic husband.

Unlike Nora, however, Mary Rockwell did not run off from husband and children to "find herself." Instead, she imploded into herself, into a mental sinkhole of alcohol and prescription drugs. Rockwell's three sons were placed in boarding school, and more and more of Mary Rockwell's time was spent in residence at the Austen Riggs Center, a psychiatric treatment center in Stockbridge, Massachusetts, sixty-two miles down Route 7 from Arlington. Increasingly, Rockwell stayed over in Stockbridge at the Red Lion Inn, just catty-corner from Austin Riggs.

Then in 1953, literally overnight, they packed up their family belongings, put their Vermont house up for sale, and moved to Stockbridge, Massachusetts. They never did say goodbye to their Arlington neighbors, nor to their friends across the river in Washington County.

ᔕ

Ostensibly, Rockwell moved to Stockbridge, Massachusetts to secure intensive psychiatric treatment for his wife. In fact, both he and Mary were pursuing psychotherapeutic care in the tiny Berkshire community.

Rockwell was suffering from depression. In his autobiography, the illustrator confessed, "I sank deeper into the muck. I was dissatisfied, doubted my ability; decisions made in the morning evaporated by three o'clock." But in Stockbridge: ". . . I got to talking with Erik H. Erikson, a psychoanalyst on the staff of Austin Riggs Center. Sort of casually to begin with, but pretty soon I found myself seeing him regularly. He helped me understand the crisis. And I came through it rather more easily than I would have plodding along by myself. I sure owe a lot to Erik Erikson."

In these sessions with Erikson, Norman Rockwell began to uncover a deep, significant root to his distress: his still unfulfilled desire to "do something important". Equally troubling was his anger at the suppression of that desire by his bosses at the *Saturday Evening Post.* Dealing with this anger would require fresh starts. The village of Stockbridge, Massachusetts provided one of them.

ᔕ

Austin Riggs Center sits on a bucolic, open campus diagonally across the street from the famous Red Lion Inn in the quintessential New England village of Stockbridge. Although very old and very historic, The Red Lion, opened in 1773, is nowhere near as old as Stockbridge itself.

The village was settled as a Christian mission to the Mohican Indian tribe in 1734, and the second minister to serve the Native American community was the noted puritan preacher and theologian Jonathan Edwards. When Edwards arrived in "Indian Town" from his previous home in Northampton, Massachusetts, he brought with him his manservant, a free black man named Agrippa Hull.

During the Revolutionary War, Hull served as valet to the heralded freedom fighter, General Thaddeus Kosciusko. Returning to Stockbridge, Agrippa Hull married a free black woman named Jane, and took a position in the home of Theodore Sedgwick. Sedgwick was the activist Stockbridge lawyer who had won the "freedom suit" for slave Elizabeth Freeman, thus effectively abolishing slavery in the state of Massachusetts.

Agrippa Hull became the largest black landowner in Stockbridge, and a prominent and well-respected resident. (A portrait of and memorial to Hull now hangs in the Stockbridge Historical Society Museum.) At some point, Agrippa and Jane adopted an abandoned mixed race child from New York State whose name was Mary Gunn.

Norman Rockwell and the Gunn Family of Stockbridge, MA

Characteristic of the diversity and tolerance that characterized this picture-postcard village since its founding, the citizens of Stockbridge, Massachusetts matter-of-factly shared their cafes, shops and services with patients from Austin Riggs Psychiatric Center and tourists from The Red Lion Inn. When Norman Rockwell was ready to try again to break out and do something more than "grandfathers and puppy dogs," he had no trouble finding models of color to help him do it. For one thing, he and David Gunn, a direct descendant of Mary Gunn, were pipe-smoking buddies.

The Gunn family was eighth-generation African-American residents of Stockbridge, Massachusetts. In the 1960's, David Gunn, Sr., was athletic director at The Lenox School, the first black man to hold such a post at a white private school in New England.

Gunn, being a member of one of the oldest families of the village, helped Rockwell the newcomer to get to know who was who among his long-established Stockbridge neighbors: "He called me Dave and I called him Norman, and he'd tell me he was looking for someone with a certain facial expression. So I'd look around and find someone for him, and it usually worked." Those Stockbridge faces went on to become some of the most memorable characters in American art.

❧

For six years, with the help of neighbors like David Gunn and the support of the Austin Riggs staff, Norman Rockwell painted some of his most memorable Saturday Evening Post Covers from his studio over the butcher shop on Main Street in Stockbridge, Massachusetts. Then a family tragedy changed everything.

On August 25, 1959, Mary Barstow Rockwell died from heart failure while napping in their Stockbridge home. Two years previously, she had been admitted to the Institute for Living in Hartford, Connecticut, a psychiatric center specializing in electroconvulsive therapy. Austen Riggs had concluded Mary was too ill for its open environment. Her long-term abuse of alcohol combined with psycho-pharmaceutical drugs and electric shock treatments may have triggered Mary Rockwell's death at the early age of fifty-one.

Norman Rockwell continued his sessions with Erik Erickson, the two eventually becoming close friends. Erickson continued to encourage Rockwell to find a way to make "the big statements" that roiled around inside him.

In the autumn of 1960, it was Erikson who brought home to Rockwell the depth of a drama unfolding in the American South. Erikson's associate and fellow psychologist, Robert Cole, was in New Orleans volunteering as a therapist for a little girl named Ruby Bridges. Cole told his colleague in Stockbridge the story of Ruby Bridges and Erik Erickson, in turn, told the story to Norman Rockwell.

Walking To School: The Story of Ruby, Pam and Yvonne

On November 14, 1960, Ruby Bridges, a six-year-old black girl, was walking to school –William Frantz Elementary School in New Orleans, Louisiana, to be exact. Her walk took her through screaming mobs of white segregationists hurling racial epithets, and worse.

And Ruby wasn't the only little girl braving hate-filled mobs as she valiantly walked to school that day. Two little white girls were also running the same gauntlet. Five-year-old Pam Foreman stepped out assuredly under the protective arm of her father, the Reverend Lloyd Foreman. Six-year-old Yvonne Gabrielle, whose father was overseas in the service, moved more timidly, leaning into the encircling embrace of her mother, Daisy.

Neither white parent, Daisy Gabrielle nor Lloyd Foreman, was a radical or activist of any kind. Foreman, a minister and war veteran just decided that he wasn't going to let any mob tell him what to do. Mrs. Gabrielle, a former Women's Army Corps member whose husband had spent three years in foxholes in New Guinea, simply said, "It was the principle of the thing."

Their separate gauntlet walks over, the three little girls remained segregated once inside the school building. Each child was taught in a separate classroom, even though Ruby and Yvonne were both first graders. Ruby was blessed to have Mrs. Barbara Henry for her instructor. Henry, a brand-new teacher from Boston, Massachusetts, had been the only member of the William Frantz faculty willing to teach a black child.

Ruby, Gabrielle and Yvonne each recollect feeling terribly alone during those long school days. "I thought at first that there *were* no other kids," Bridges recalls, remembering how she finally heard other children in the hallway one day and longed to find them and play.

Little kindergartener Pam Foreman also knew there were other kids in the school and she wanted to play with them, too. She'd seen the Gabrielle family walking to William Franz, and she also knew that there was a black girl named Ruby somewhere in the building. One time in the hall, Pam peeked through pane-glass windows, saw Bridges, and was chastised by her white teachers for doing so. Finally, in the spring of 1961, after pressure had been put on the school administration from Barbara Henry, the children were allowed to play together during recess.

On that first day of class in November, 1960, William Franz Elementary School had an enrollment of 2000 students, most of them walking to school. By the end of the first week, the school's rolls show only three students making that walk. Three little girls–one black, two white–whose parents were determined to do what was right.

ℭ

When he heard the Ruby Bridges story, Norman Rockwell wanted to do what was right as well. He was agitated and incensed, telling Erik Erikson that the scenes of violence in New Orleans reported daily on the nightly news disturbed him deeply.

Rockwell wanted to tell the story unfolding in New Orleans the best way he knew how: with his art. But the famous illustrator was still under contract with the *Saturday Evening Post*, and the *Post* still held firmly to its unwritten code: "colored people" could appear in the publication only in menial tasks. Erik Erickson started to suggest more directly that, for his mental health, maybe it was time for Norman Rockwell to leave *The Saturday Evening Post*. Rockwell wasn't quite ready to take that momentous step. But he did take another one.

ɞ

On October 25, 1961, Norman Rockwell married Mary "Molly" Punderson in a private ceremony at St. Paul Episcopal Church in Stockbridge. Rockwell had met Molly while attending a poetry class she taught at the Lenox Massachusetts Public Library. A retired school teacher of old Yankee stock, Molly was matter-of-fact, independent, liberal and an activist. Her whole persona was an elixir for the discouraged artist. Molly Punderson Rockwell joined Erik Erikson in urging her new husband to break out and move on. Finally, after two years of waffling, he did just that.

ɞ

In the fall of 1963, Norman Rockwell informed *The Saturday Evening Post* that effective January, 1964, his affiliation with the publication was over. The famous illustrator was going to work for *Look*, a magazine whose more liberal policies would allow expression of his beliefs regarding human rights and tolerance. The first expression he planned to make was about Ruby Bridges walking to school. He would call the painting, "The Problem We All Live With"

Modeling "The Problem We All Live With"

It appears Rockwell began working on "The Problem We All Live With" sometime during the autumn of 1963, while he was still at *The Saturday Evening Post* but after he had given notice of his departure. The more Rockwell saw the press footage of the little black girl walking among the big white Federal marshals, the more convinced he was of the image he wished to capture. And Rockwell knew exactly where to find black models for that image: his buddy David Gunn's granddaughters, Anita and Lynda Gunn.

෴

Anita Gunn still clearly remembers how, on a street in her home town of Great Barrington, Massachusetts, Norman Rockwell literally walked into her life. "It was the fall of 1963. I was coming home from school, crying because I wanted to take violin lessons. I loved watching our music teacher play and I wanted to learn. But my parents said we couldn't afford the $25 for the lessons."

As Anita sniffled along the street, a tall white man approached her, asking what was wrong. When the 8-year-old explained that she wanted to take violin lessons but there was no money for them, the man suggested that, if her mother approved, he would pay for the lessons if Anita would model for him.

"I didn't understand anything about modeling. All I heard was $25! I had no idea who he was. And I didn't tell my mother."

It seems Norman Rockwell had recognized the crying child as one of David Gunn's granddaughters and decided, while comforting her, to make his modeling pitch right then and there.

At this point, the narration of the story switches over to Elaine Scott Gunn, Anita's mother. Several days after the sidewalk encounter described above, Elaine Gunn remained home from her teaching job at the local elementary school to care for one of Anita's brothers, who was sick. When Mrs. Gunn heard a knock at her front door, she opened it only to find Norman Rockwell standing on the stoop.

Gunn immediately recognized the famous illustrator, although she had never met him. Rockwell introduced himself, explaining that he had come from Stockbridge, eight miles away, to talk with her daughter, Anita.

Mrs. Gunn, stunned at the presence of this national icon on her doorstep, stammered that Anita was not yet home from school.

"May I wait for her?" Rockwell politely requested.

When Anita finally tromped through the backdoor, she found her mother sitting at the dining room table, chatting with the man who had spoken to her on the street.

As the little girl entered the room, Norman Rockwell rose and approached her. Stooping down and clasping her hands, he asked, "How would you like to earn money for those violin lessons?" Then, according to Mrs. Gunn, Rockwell engaged the 8-year-old in a discussion about his latest project on the subject of integration.

Only when Anita, in her blue, Peter Pan-collared school dress, understood what "modeling" meant and what she was agreeing to did the artist turn back to Mrs. Gunn: "For the modeling session, can you have two dresses made just like the one she has on, only in white?"

The other dress was for Lynda Gunn, Anita's cousin who lived back in Stockbridge, and who Rockwell planned on using as a model, as well.

Several weeks later, on a sunny Sunday morning, Anita Gunn, her father Clarence, mother Elaine and three siblings all piled into the family station wagon for the drive over to Norman Rockwell's studio in Stockbridge. Rockwell had invited the entire family to come over for Anita's modeling session and, even though it meant missing church (not an inconsequential matter for these staunch Congregationalists), nobody wanted to miss it. For this special occasion, everybody was in their Sunday best anyway, including Anita in her special white dress. Elaine Gunn recalls the keyed-up children wriggling around in the back seat and her trying to calm them so they wouldn't ruin their outfits during the fifteen-minute ride.

When the Gunn clan arrived at the studio, they found that Norman Rockwell had set up chairs for each of them. Once they were settled, the famous illustrator then went to a case of Coca Cola he kept under the stairs leading to a loft in the studio, and proceeded to open and hand a bottle of Coke to each member of the group.

"It was wonderful," Anita Gunn, now Tinsley, remembers with a laugh. "We didn't have to share. We each had our own bottle."

During the modeling session, Anita was required to stand absolutely still, with her feet positioned on wooden blocks for long minutes at a time. When Rockwell guided her poses, he bent down and spoke to the little girl directly. "He was very kind," Tinsley recalls. The session lasted about 45 minutes, and at its conclusion, the little model received a check for $25, signed by Norman Rockwell.

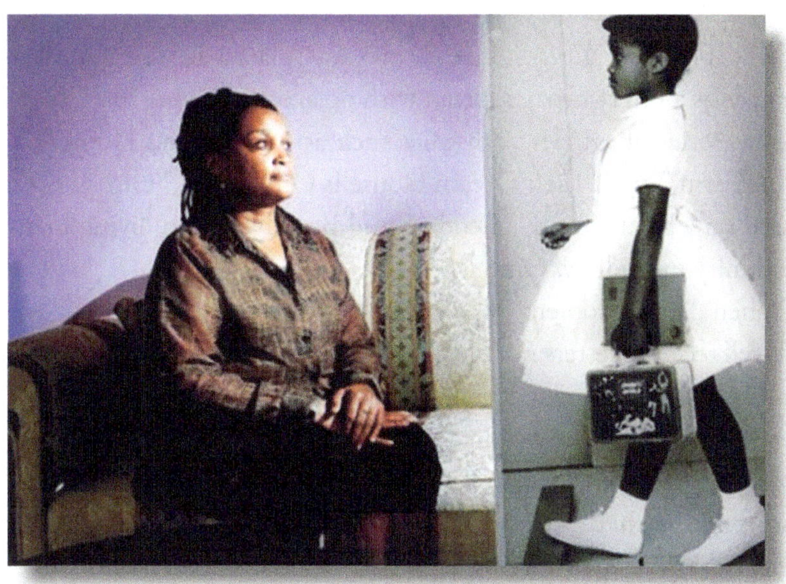

Anita Gunn Tinsley

"The Problem We All Live With" appeared in the January 14, 1964 edition of *Look* magazine. It was Rockwell's first work for the publication. The illustration depicts six-year-old Ruby Bridges surrounded by a phalanx of federal marshals, walking to school. In the 36-inches high by 58-inches wide oil painting, only the marshals' torsos are shown–no faces–creating a feeling of menace. The little student strides along, clutching her books, eyes straight forward, while on the wall behind her is scrawled the racial epithet "NIGGER" and the letters, "KKK." The bright red blotch of a smashed tomatoes blossoms just over her head.

The January 14, 1964 edition of *Look* did not feature "The Problem We All Live With" as its cover, nor make any mention of Norman Rockwell. Rather, it featured photos of American homes in various urban and suburban settings, along with family shots highlighting the cover story: "How We Live: Up in the city, Down on the farm, Out in the suburbs. In homes packed with pride, prejudice and love."

"The Problem We All Live With" was placed in the middle of the magazine as a full two-page spread with no accompanying text. It appeared amidst a series of articles with titles such as: "Their First Home," "Down On the Farm," and "Their Dream House Is On Wheels." One of the stories focused on a black family, Theodore and Beverly Mason, living in a mixed community in Ludlow, Ohio.

When "The Problem We All Live With" hit the stands, Norman Rockwell received letters not only of praise but also of criticism from readers unused to seeing such direct social commentary flow from the easel of their favorite artist. But Rockwell had turned a corner and he did not turn back. Stephanie Plunkett, Norman Rockwell Museum deputy director and chief curator, noting that this was the first painting purchased by the museum, observes that the "painting ushered in a new era in Rockwell's career, and remains an important national symbol of the struggle for racial equality."

"The Problem We All Live With" chronicles an historic breakthrough in America's civil rights struggle. For Norman Rockwell, it represented a critical victory in his struggles as an artist, as well. And the catalyst for it all was little Ruby Bridges. But "The Problem We All Live With" is not a painting of Ruby Bridges. It is a portrait of Anita Gunn, in composite with her cousin Lynda Gunn.

Fading From Plain Sight

Most people don't have a clue who the little girl(s) in "The Problem We All Live With" really is(are). Even Ron Schick, award-winning author of *Norman Rockwell: Behind The Camera*, got things mixed up. In his book, Schick states that the composite image is of three, not two, children (whom he does not name). "I tried to tell him (Schick) that there were just two models, Anita and Lynda," Elaine Gunn, Anita's mother and Lynda's aunt explained to me. "Of the three photos used in his book, two are of Lynda, one with her braids down and one with them pinned up. But I guess he didn't hear me."

ᘓ

Not being heard doesn't surprise Anita Gunn Tinsley, Elaine's daughter. Now a fifty-five year old widow living in Lynchburg, Virginia with her adult Downs Syndrome daughter, Tinsley recalls that when her other daughter, Kenita, told classmates her mother was a Norman Rockwell model, they thought she was nuts. Tinsley had to send Kenita back to school with proof to stop the scoffing. "That was typical," Anita Gunn Tinsley recalls. "I really don't bother telling people about it anymore."

ꕥ

Norman Rockwell model Anita Gunn Tinsley has never seen the actual painting of "The Problem We All Live With." In fact, she had no idea of the painting's significance until she attended a Rockwell models' reunion at The Norman Rockwell Museum in Stockbridge in 2007. There, 44 years after her modeling session, Tinsley learned of the immense importance of the picture she had posed for. Before returning home to Virginia, she went to the museum's bookstore and bought a reproduction of the iconic illustration, which now hangs in her bedroom.

"I'm not one to show myself," Anita Tinsley told me. "But to know I'm seen by millions of people, seeing myself, it's a strange feeling."

ꕥ

"The Problem We All Live With" was back in the national spotlight recently. To mark the fiftieth anniversary of the integration of America's segregated public school systems in the South, President Barack Obama borrowed the famous work from the Norman Rockwell Museum and hung it outside the entrance to the Oval Office, where he can see it from his desk. When I informed Anita that her likeness is now on the wall directly outside of the Oval Office, her first reaction was, "Wow!" Then stunned silence. After a moment, she whispered, "Maybe I'll try to take a trip to Washington to see it." I didn't have the heart to tell her that admission to the Oval Office was not that easy to come by, even if you are a Norman Rockwell model, one of the "little black girl(s) in the white dress."

ꕥ

And what about the other little model for "The Problem We All Live With," Anita's cousin, Lynda? Lynda Gunn is now night auditor for a small motel in western Massachusetts, not far from her hometown of Stockbridge.

Like Ruby Bridges, Lynda Gunn had been the only black child in her elementary school. However, she was a Gunn of the eight generations of Stockbridge Gunns. Her grandfather, David Gunn, Sr., was a well-known and respected figure in the community. "It was a very sheltered experience," Lynda recalled. I just got to be a child."

Although her parents were racially proud members of the N.A.A.C.P., Lynda did not experience any racism until she was in high school. Only one time during her elementary school days does she remember feeling different. Her class began reading "Little Black Sambo." "Everybody turned around and looked at me," she said. "But it wasn't traumatic."

As an adult, she found that her Yankee accent provided a measure of cultural camouflage. "I've gotten a lot of job interviews–on the phone, it's one thing, but when I show up, the jaws drop," she said.

Lynda's father, David Gunn, Jr. accompanied her to Norman Rockwell's studio for her photo shoot. She, too, wore a white dress made to Norman Rockwell's specifications by the dressmaker friend of Lynda's Aunt Elaine. As he did with her cousin Anita, Rockwell worked at getting the little Lynda's Keds-shod feet balanced just right on wooden blocks to give her body the posture of walking. Photos show her dad with a straight-armed hand flat against her back, trying to keep her aligned.

But Lynda was not Anita. "I was a real wiseacre," only child Lynda Gunn confided to me with a lopsided grin. Uncomfortable and bored, Lynda began making faces and complaining to the famous illustrator. Her father was mortified but, Lynda recalls, Norman Rockwell was very patient. "It was easy to be myself with him."

Unlike her cousin Anita, who left western Massachusetts as a teenager, Lynda Gunn never left the Berkshire region. Thus, she was fully aware of the importance of "The Problem We All Live With" and the international recognition held by the little figure who is central in it.

Lynda has been interviewed by David Brinkley and featured in articles published in local and regional newspapers and magazines. But as honored as she is to have played a part in the creation of this painting, Gunn admits she would have preferred royalties over the ten dollars per session she was paid by Norman Rockwell. (It seems Anita Gunn's twenty-five dollar payment was special.) Lynda also feels it would have been nice if she and Anita had been invited to the White House to view the painting, like Ruby Bridges was. "But I wasn't expecting anything, so I'm not disappointed," Gunn said.

In fact, Norman Rockwell model Lynda Gunn has largely stopped participating in events involving "The Problem We All Live With." Echoing Washington County Rockwell model Paul Adams, she declares, "It got to be too much: 'Will you come and sign autographs?' for nothing. So I stopped."

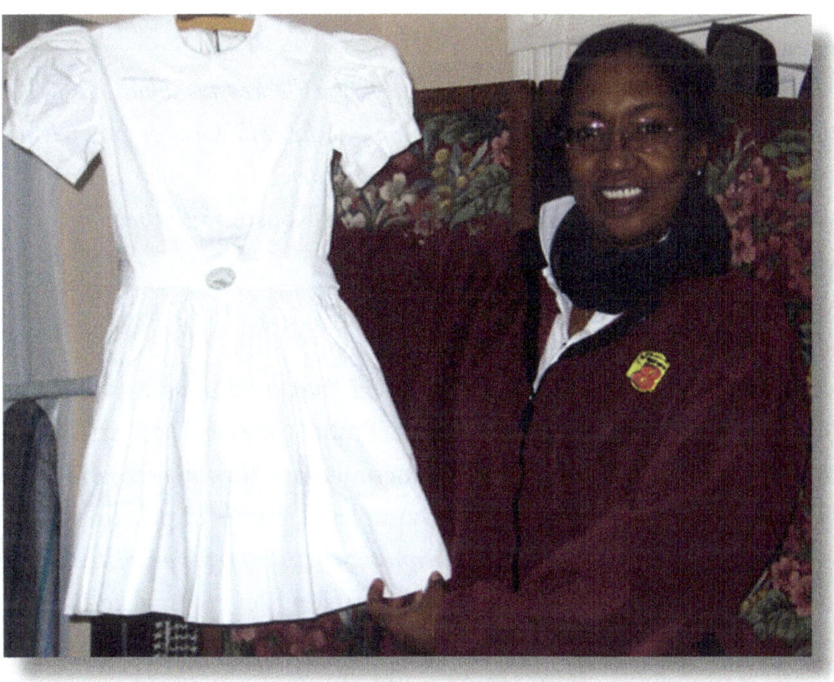

Lynda Gunn, Holding Dress in Which She Modeled for "The Problem We All Live With"

The Strange Encounter of A Celebrity Chef, The Pop Artist and The Norman Rockwell Model

Riddle: What do celebrity chef Marcus Samuelsson, contemporary pop artist Philip Maysles and Norman Rockwell all have in common? Answer: admiration for the profile of eight-year-old Lynda Gunn.

In September, 2011, a few weeks after meeting with Lynda Gunn in her hometown in the Berkshires, I took a Metro North train down to 125th Street in Harlem. Mission: get my bi-annual hit of soul food and have a catch up lady chat with my longtime friend and sister Barnard alumna, Laverne Trawick. We agreed to succumb to the media hype, forego the tried and true Sylvia's Restaurant, *and give the newly-acclaimed* Red Rooster Restaurant *a try. The luminary-packed Harlem restaurant, touted as one of New York's hottest new eateries, was owned and operated by Marcus Samuelsson, one of the world's hottest celebrity chefs.*

As we waited in the bar area for a table, LaV asked me what was the latest with "the Rockwell project" (as it had come to be called among my friends). I was describing Lynda Gunn and her poignant perspective when Laverne and I were escorted into the dining room of The Red Rooster *and there, all over the walls, was Lynda Gunn.*

❧

Marcus Samuelsson (owner of *The Red Rooster*, famous chef and a black Harlem resident) is close friends with Philip Maysles (pop artist, son of Albert Maysles the award-winning documentary film maker, and a white Harlem resident). In 2006, Maysles completed a series of paintings entitled *The Comfort of Enlightenment, an iconoclastic interpretation of the Norman Rockwell narrative.* In explaining the series, Maysles commented, "A lot of my work is exploring white identity, and how whiteness is constructed in relation to images people have of black folk".

Originally displayed at The Museum of Fine Arts in Houston in the autumn of 2011, the five huge canvases graced the walls of the *Red Rooster Restaurant* in Harlem. Lynda Gunn's profile appears in all five.

In one painting, for example, Philip Maysles has drawn Gunn, schoolbooks in hand, being carefully positioned by her father, David Gunn,

Jr., while posing in Norman Rockwell's studio. The most striking painting in the series is a rendering of Norman Rockwell's famous self-portrait. In Maysles' version, Rockwell's face on the canvas has been replaced by Lynda Gunn's profile. Philip Maysles has commented that this work is his own oblique self-portrait.

☙

The wait staff at *The Red Rooster* did not know if I was a seriously disgruntled customer, an extremely pleased one, a heavy-duty undercover restaurant critic, a crazy woman, or all of the above: I patiently, politely but persistently insisted on speaking with Marcus Samuelsson. My friend Laverne, who had been watching all of this with growing amusement (she knows me well), broke into a big grin when the famous chef, complete in "dress whites," finally appeared at our table. Within the two minutes of my pop interview, Marcus Samuelsson found out who Lynda Gunn was, gave me contact information for Philip Maysles and invited us all back to the restaurant.

☙

Until I told her about it, Lynda Gunn had never heard of The Red Rooster *restaurant. She had no idea who Philip Maysles was, nor did she know that her likeness was all over the walls of the restaurant, one of the most "see and be seen" places in New York City.*

In the afternoon of October 31, 2011, I drove from my home in Woodstock, New York to the Berkshires to pick up Lynda Gunn. She was going to spend the night with me in Woodstock and the next day we would take the train down to Harlem and lunch at The Red Rooster. *The publicity mavens had been at work: Rebecca Mead, esteemed senior writer for* New Yorker *magazine was joining us. Her story would chronicle the Harlem encounter of the pop artist, the night clerk and the celebrity chef, all brought together by Norman Rockwell.*

Lynda and I had a wonderful home cooked style meal of liver, onions and bacon at The Red Onion *restaurant in Woodstock that night before traveling to New York, then turning in early, excited about the big day coming up. The next day we descended the stairs from the Metro North platform onto 125th street, "country girls" taking in all the sights, sounds and smells of the African village that is 125th Street.*

As we walked crosstown to Lenox Avenue and the restaurant, Lynda was enthralled with the street vendor jewelry, the giant jars of cocoa butter, the hair braiding shops and soul food restaurants. By the time we got to The Red Rooster, *we were ready for a good fill of soul food.*

We were greeted outside the front door of The Red Rooster by Philip Maysles, a tall, thin, earnest young man who immediately thanked us profusely for coming. He expressed to Lynda his deep excitement at seeing and actually meeting the model who had inspired his paintings. As we walked into the main dining room, Maysles urged Lynda to be honest with him in her reactions to his work. Rebecca Mead quietly joined us at that point, introduced herself, and began taking notes.

Lynda walked around the restaurant, looking at each painting. As she did so, some restaurant patrons glanced at her, then at the paintings on the wall, then back at her. A buzz started around the room.

Philip and Lynda chatted as she studied each painting. The two of them seemed to really bond. At one point I overheard Philip ask Lynda, "Have I done anything with these paintings that might be offensive to you?" I didn't hear Lynda's answer, but I did see Philip's intensity soften just a bit as their heads came together again in a flow of conversation.

At another point, Maysles asked, "Do you feel resentment toward me?" This time I did hear the answer. "I'm not resentful," Gunn responded quietly. "I'm happy to see you went somewhere with it."

Having completed our gallery walk of the paintings, the four of us, Lynda, Philip, Rebecca and I, were seated at a reserved table towards the back of the dining room. Then Marcus Samuelsson, complete with entourage of publicity assistants and camera persons, swept onto the scene.

Complimentary pumpkin soup and macaroni-and-cheese were placed before us as Samuelsson grasped Lynda's hands in both of his, welcoming her profusely. Cameras flashed as the vaunted chef posed with the Rockwell model while presenting her with one of his hefty cookbooks. I caught Lynda's eye: she did not look happy.

Then Samuelsson and his staff swept out of the dining room, greeting various trendy patrons as they went. Although Philip had been recognized and, in fact, commandeered into one of the photos, neither Rebecca Mead nor I had received the briefest "hello."

Unfortunately for Lynda's and my rumbling stomachs, the food wasn't that good, either. The "complimentary" soup was too spicy, and the chicken salad Lynda ordered was too salty. Philip Maysles paid the tab for us all.

Later, Lynda would tell me she felt a palpable difference between Maysles and Marcus. "A question of genuineness," she said.

As we left The Red Rooster, *Lynda and Philip hugged goodbye. Then Maysles asked her if she would sign a postcard-size reproduction of his "Self-Portrait of Norman Rockwell as Ruby Bridges" which he had brought along with him. Lynda Gunn signed it, then boldly wrote her name across the blue shirtsleeve of the artist's painting arm.*

As Lynda and I hurried back across 125th Street to the Metro North station, our stomachs protested every time we passed one of its aromatic ethnic restaurants. Visions of the *liver and bacon feast from the night before floated in our heads.*

Our train ride back to Poughkeepsie was quiet, reflective. Lynda said she was sad about The Red Rooster: *"I wanted to like the place. And I was really looking forward to a good meal."*

I said that I had felt like one of Norman Rockwell's "other people": hidden in plain sight, invisible.

We picked up my car at the train station and headed up to the Berkshires. As we exited the Mass Pike near Lynda's house, she asked if we could stop for some food because "I am so hungry!" I said, "Me, too!" and we made a sharp U-turn right into the local McDonald's.

Chapter 5

THE OTHERS IN "THE GOLDEN RULE"

"We are the governed, but we govern too."
Look Magazine, August, 1968

A disheartened Norman Rockwell had turned his sketch of the United Nations to the wall when he was back at his Arlington studio. Now, in his Stockbridge studio, Rockwell was ready to try his "big picture" again. The social and political climate of 1961 was perfect for it: JFK had just been inaugurated, Amnesty International had just been organized, and the civil rights movement was ramping up in the South.

Even *The Saturday Evening Post* had loosened up a bit, sensing that their prized pony was chafing at the bit and about to bolt. "The Golden Rule", published on the cover of *The Saturday Evening Post* on April Fool's Day, 1961, marked a turning point in Norman Rockwell's relationship with *The Saturday Evening Post.* Finally following his conscience, Rockwell stepped out and integrated *The Post* covers all by himself.

❧

"Do unto others. . ." For most Americans in 1961, that familiar "golden rule" really meant, "Do unto others who look like *you*." Norman Rockwell's "Golden Rule" challenged that hypocrisy and laid the truth of "the other" smack dab in the middle of America's coffee tables.

The illustrator resurrected the "peoples of the world" theme from his United Nations mural. But the models for the figures in "The Golden Rule" were all *local* people–Rockwell's friends, acquaintances and neighbors in Stockbridge and from his Arlington days–a fact that reveals the panorama of "others" who were a part of Norman Rockwell's life.

The Rainbow of Models in The Golden Rule

The little black girl gazing out from the bottom left corner of the painting, hands folded in prayer, is Pauline Adams. To the right above her, in the direct center of the painting, is her brother, Paul Adams. Continuing on that diagonal, we encounter the direct scrutiny of David Gunn, Jr., eldest son David, Sr., Rockwell's pipe-smoking buddy.

But "The Golden Rule" did not introduce just African-American subjects to the cover of *The Saturday Evening Post*. The brown girl in the red shawl, right below Paul Adams in the illustration, is Darlene Simon, niece to Michael Abdalla, Stockbridge's Lebanese grocer. (Members of two of Stockbridge's old guard families, the Abdalla and Gunn kids attended school together.)

Michael and his wife, Judy, owned the Elm Street Market, gathering place not only for groceries but equally important for coffee, a sandwich and the latest local news and analysis. Although it is now owned and operated by Russians and Brazilians, The Elm Street Market has barely changed since Norman Rockwell hung out there. The original counter and stools appear to be still there. The original menu (or at least what reads like it) is still there, complete with a grilled cheese sandwich on plain old Wonder Bread-type white bread. It even looks like (hygiene buffs, take note) the original grill is still there. The Elm Street Market is a wonderful place.

During one of his visits to Elm Street, Norman Rockwell apparently looked more closely at the striking features of its proprietor and invited Michael Abdalla to model for him. Abdalla's face appears twice in "The Golden Rule," peering out from both left and right of center at the top of the painting.

It may have been during the photo shoot with the market owner that Norman Rockwell mentioned he was looking for a brown baby to model for his latest work. Michael Abdalla introduced his sister, Coreen Abdalla Nejame, and her son, his little nephew Scott, to the famous illustrator.

Coreen Nejame, also a Stockbridge native and a fourth-grade school teacher, remembers carrying her infant son to the famous artist's studio. Nejame was surprised to learn that Rockwell wanted her to model as well, but he didn't like the sweater she was wearing. Rummaging around in his props, Rockwell pulled out a long shawl which he carefully draped around the mother and her infant son. Then the photo shoot began. Scott Nejame, now a New York State judge, holds the dubious distinction of being a Rockwell model immortalized wearing a diaper and shawl.

Another member of Stockbridge's Lebanese community appearing in "The Golden Rule" is Michael Abdalla's niece, Darlene Simon. Standing just below Paul Adams, Darlene is the beautiful dusky maiden in the red shawl, although her aunt, Judy Abdalla, hastens to assert that, in reality, Darlene "is not that dark. Rockwell colored her in. He did that, you know."

❧

In addition to Lebanese and African-Americans, "The Golden Rule" is, as far as I can tell, the only Norman Rockwell illustration that includes Asian-American models. According to records in the Norman Rockwell Archives and Library, May Jeu, Paul Fong and Fooknew Yip were each paid models for Norman Rockwell. Peter Fung, in fact, had two photo shoots at the Stockbridge studio, one on August 21, 1960 and another on September 25, 1960, the same day Michael Abdalla posed for his photos.

Although a very tolerant place, it does not appear that Stockbridge was home to any of these Asian families. Most likely, Norman Rockwell found Mary, Paul and Fooknew through his contacts in the neighboring town of North Adams, Massachusetts. North Adams has been home to a community of Asian residents since 1870.

❧

In April, 1870, employees of the Calvin T. Sampson Shoe Factory, one of the largest employers in North Adams at the time, struck for higher wages and against the ten-hour workday. Calvin T. Sampson (C.T. to his friends) fired them all.

The intrepid industrialist then proceeded to bring in replacement workers from nearby towns. However, the burly Scottish and Irish strikers, all members of the powerful Knights of Saint Crispin, persuaded the out-of-towners not to stay.

At that point, C.T. Sampson sent his factory superintendent, George W. Chase, to San Francisco with instructions to find and employ "75 steady, active and intelligent Chinamen," offering them contracts for three years. Chase followed orders, and on a warm June morning in 1870, seventy-five Chinese workers stepped off the train in North Adams, Massachusetts. The "men" were between the ages of fourteen and twenty-two years old. Only one of the group, Charles Sing, was able to speak English.

They had contracted to work eleven-hour workdays (ten-and-a-half in the fall and winter) for 90 cents a day, less than half of the strikers' wages. In addition to housing, the agreement allowed for a small increase in pay during the second and third years. C.T. Sampson agreed to pay the return fare to California for any man who worked the full three years or more. Sampson was the first American manufacturer to transport Chinese workers east of the Rockies to break a strike.

Under the protection of a private police force, the Chinese arrivals threaded their way through a hostile mob from Union Depot in North Adams to their living quarters next to the Sampson factory. Then, incredibly, their new employer marched them back out of the building, lined the new workers up along the south wall of his factory, and photographed the group. Nearly one hundred years later, Chinese residents of North Adams were again being photographed, but this time as models for Norman Rockwell's "Golden Rule."

ꟹ

Unlike the United Nations sketch, "The Golden Rule" portrays no world leaders and nobody is waiting for anybody to straighten out anything. Instead, each of us is looking directly into the faces of all of us: young, old, black, white, brown, male, female. We are each "the other," responsible *to* each other for the world we create. Years before Zucotti Park, Norman Rockwell painted the 99%.

ꟹ

Soon after "The Golden Rule" appeared as a *Saturday Evening Post* cover, Norman Rockwell was presented with the Interfaith Award from the National Conference of Christians and Jews. The citation recognized the internationally-known artist for "his dedication to the highest ideals of amity, understanding, and cooperation among men." His Interfaith Award was one of Norman Rockwell's most treasured possessions.

Finally, Rockwell had been able to paint "a big idea" with "a big picture". It felt good, it felt right. So he left *The Saturday Evening Post*, went to *Look* magazine, and proceeded to illustrate the '60's.

Chapter 6

MODELING THE 60'S

"To hell with the magazines, my responsibilities."
Norman Rockwell

A major influence on Norman Rockwell's choice of subjects in the 1960's was his friend and confidant, the psychiatrist Erik Erikson. Erikson was a student of racial prejudice and its effects on personality. Much of the evidence for the landmark desegregation decision, "Brown vs. The Board of Education," was based on Erikson's 1950 book, *Childhood and Society.* Through Erikson's work and that of his colleague, Robert Cole, psychology became the country's conscience.

For Norman Rockwell, this consciousness was liberating. As an article in the December, 1970 issue of *Good Housekeeping* magazine put it, two Rockwells now presented themselves to the world: *The Saturday Evening Post* Rockwell of praying grandmothers and the *Look* magazine Rockwell of social problems and politics.

When Rockwell went over to *Look* magazine, he embraced that publication's commitment to covering contemporary issues: racial intolerance, space exploration, suburban integration, the Peace Corps–subjects that were taboo at the *Post.* And as Frank Paddock, one of the doctors at Austin Riggs, observed, Rockwell's paintings in the sixties often expressed despair over an imperfect America rarely revealed on the covers of *The Saturday Evening Post.* In many of these paintings, the illustrator included people of color.

Modeling Civil Rights for Norman Rockwell

"The Problem We All Live With" appeared in January, 1964. Norman Rockwell's next two comments on an imperfect America were published the following year. "How Goes The War On Poverty" was published in the July 27, 1965 issue of *Look*, accompanying an article of the same name written by Sargent Shriver. Under the illustration, the caption reads: "The poor are cynical. They have been exploited, and they know it. They are wary of new programs."

"How Goes The War On Poverty" features two "helping hands," both white, one pulling up the other. In the background a specter of skeptical faces is watching. Two of those faces are black: Paul and Pauline Adams. Norman Rockwell utilized the "face shots" he had taken of the children at their home in Washington Country nearly ten years before. However, for his next statement on social justice, "Mississippi Justice," Rockwell knew he would have to use models who were much more contemporary.

ᔓ

On a moonlit night in June, 1964, Michael Schwerner, James Chaney and Andrew Goodman were murdered by the Ku Klux Klan. The Klan buried their bodies beneath an earthen dam on a back road outside of Philadelphia, Mississippi. Schwerner was 24 years old, Chaney was 21, and Goodman only 20.

Michael Schwerner, a white New York City social worker, had gone down to Mississippi to head up a voter registration drive organized by the Congress of Racial Equality (CORE). Andrew Goodman, a 20-year-old white anthropology student who was also from New York, was spending his summer in Mississippi as a volunteer with the drive.

James Chaney, a native of Meridian, Mississippi, was the local CORE liaison and chief aide to Schwerner. Chaney had become active in the cause early on: at the age of 15, he and his fellow black high school students had gone to their segregated school wearing paper patches reading "NAACP" to demonstrate their support for that national civil rights organization. For this, the young people were suspended from school for a week.

When Schwerner, Cheney and Goodman were reported missing, people across America responded with apprehension and fear. J. Edgar Hoover, with his antipathy to civil rights groups, resisted getting the FBI involved until President Lynden Johnson threatened him with political reprisals. So, one hundred and fifty FBI agents went to Mississippi. During their investigation, the agents discovered seven bodies of Mississippi blacks whose disappearances over the past several years had attracted attention only within their local communities. But there was no sign of the three missing men they were looking for.

Finally, Mississippi state trooper Maynard King, stepping forward to claim a $25,000 reward, offered crucial information about the case. The civil rights workers' bodies were found on August 4th, 1964. No one was charged for their deaths.

The nation was outraged–as was its favorite artist. So, on a cold morning in early March, 1965, Norman Rockwell began conceptualizing "Murder in Mississippi." Serendipitously, a few days later, *Look* magazine asked the artist to illustrate "Southern Justice," an article for its upcoming June 29th issue.

"Southern Justice" was a short story written by Alabamian Charles Morgan, Jr., a leading civil rights lawyer, often vilified by fellow whites. The story was, according to Rockwell in a personal, handwritten letter to Morgan, "an unanswerable indictment" of racial bigotry. Rockwell who, according to his son Thomas, had only two political passions–nuclear disarmament and civil rights–was honored to be asked to portray it. Work on "Murder in Mississippi" began in earnest.

The painting depicts the horror encountered by Cheney, Goodman and Schwerner, shown on an isolated dirt road in the middle of nowhere in the middle of the night–a scene lit only by an unseen torch. Goodman is portrayed lying on the ground, presumably beaten and trying, with one arm, to push himself up. Schwerner stares into the glow of his attacker's torch while trying to lift Cheney who appears beaten and near death.

Rockwell's draft sketches are in charcoal and the faces of the slain civil rights workers are abstract, indistinct. Only in the final painting do the three men take on solid form.

Three models were used for "Murder in Mississippi." The illustrator used his eldest son, Jarvis, to portray Michael Schwerner. According to records in the Norman Rockwell Archives, a young man by the name of William Champlain was paid to depict Andrew Goodman. James Cheney was modeled by a young black man named Oliver McCray.

As far as can be determined, no black family named "McCray" lived in Stockbridge at the time Rockwell was creating "Murder in Mississippi." Black Norman Rockwell model Oliver McCray, therefore, was probably recruited from another western Massachusetts town through the black family network that bonded these communities. Unfortunately, I have as yet been able to find out anything definitive about Oliver McCray.

Norman Rockwell ignored all other commissions in order to complete "Murder in Mississippi." Working at the pace of a much younger man (Rockwell was seventy years old at this time), the impassioned illustrator completed the work in five weeks. The 53" x 42" oil on canvas painting was sent to the *Look* offices on April 14, 1965.

But that was not the painting the magazine published in its June 29th issue. The editors of *Look* were more taken with one of Rockwell's initial charcoal sketches than with the finished painting. They felt this coarser version offered a more powerful, emotional interpretation of the story. And it does: the image of a young black man clinging to his white comrade while their other companion lays dying is haunting. In the 1960's, young Americans, black and white, *were* struggling together for tolerance and justice.

And Norman Rockwell knew that this struggle was not just happening in Mississippi. It was happening all around the world. That movement was perhaps best epitomized by the Peace Corps.

Modeling The Peace Corps

While the idea of a youth corps serving developing countries had floated around Washington since Harry Truman's time, the catalyst for actually launching such a group was the challenge issued by then-presidential candidate John F. Kennedy to an audience of Michigan college students. Within days of the speech, delivered on October 14, 1960, University of Michigan students had gathered over 1000 pledges to volunteer overseas.

Two weeks later, as a key element of his platform, Kennedy formally proposed a Peace Corps "of men and women who would dedicate themselves to the progress and peace of developing countries. " Rival candidate Richard Nixon was unwilling to endorse a similar proposal, calling the idea a "kiddie corps."

And when Kennedy took office in January 1961, he immediately set in motion the creation of the program. By August, the first 51 volunteers were travelling to Ghana. Within a few years, thousands of PCV's (as Peace Corp volunteers refer to themselves) were representing America around the globe. One of them was John Schaefer.

John, son of Chris and Mary Schaefer, close friends and former Arlington neighbors of Norman Rockwell, served as a Peace Corps volunteer in Debre Marcos, a small town in the Blue Nile region of Ethiopia. In 1965, he invited Norman and Molly Rockwell, the artist's third wife, to come and visit him there. But this would not be Rockwell's first foray into illustrating on an international scale.

ଓଃ

Ten years previously, *Pan American Airways* had sponsored him on a round-the-world trip, with the commission to produce illustrations for future *Pan Am* advertising. Traveling to sixteen cities, including Barcelona, Istanbul, Calcutta, Bangkok, Beirut and Tokyo, the enthusiastic illustrator filled his sketchbooks with scenes of the local people: bullfighters and priests, snake charmers, monkey tamers, Arabs and geisha girls.

But the *Pan Am* advertising executives didn't want pictures of the peoples of the world. They wanted pictures of American tourists around the world. Rockwell's own words best describe the situation:

"But when I returned home and submitted my sketchbook it was rejected," he bluntly states. "Because the agency and *Pan American* did not want pictures of strange lands and people. 'Those would only frighten tourists,' they said; 'we want pictures of smart-looking tourists sunning on smart beaches in front of smart hotels.' But that's not the kind of picture I can do. So I did nothing."

Paintings from those sketches of international models never materialized. "Maybe I'll do something with the sketches sometime," Rockwell mused. This may have been in his thoughts when he decided to visit John Schafer in Ethiopia.

The Rockwells were impressed with many things on this trip: Ethiopia's sights, its sounds and colors. But most of all, Norman Rockwell was impressed with the Peace Corps volunteers themselves. Here was a living actualization of the "big idea" that had been driven him for so long:

"Isn't a Peace Corps picture the answer? Youthful dedication. Something bigger than yourself. Maybe not art but my only answer, not some magazine or art editor or publicity but of my own free will."

It seems, even at *Look*, Norman Rockwell was concerned about holding onto his integrity. The artist continues:

"Not the Peace Corps one that Allen (Hurlburt, the art editor of *Look*) likes but the one I like and believe in. . . ."

ꟹ

The Peace Corps Norman Rockwell liked and believed in appeared as the *Look* magazine cover of June 14, 1966. In the painting, President Kennedy is portrayed gazing off into the light of the future, flanked by eight similarly focused young people.

John Schafer is positioned in the center of the group. In fact, according to Barry Hillenbrand, PCV alumnus and John Schafer's housemate in Debre Marcos, Norman Rockwell made the trip to Ethiopia, in part, to sketch John Schafer on location. Hillenbrand observes, "John's likeness is among those of several PCVs in the Rockwell Peace Corps picture. . ." Rockwell did use other Peace Corps volunteers as models for the painting. But the black woman the artist chose to place prominently in the upper right corner of "The Peace Corps" painting was not one of them.

ꟹ

Not very many black Americans were signed up with the Peace Corps in 1965. If a young black person wished to volunteer his or her services for the improvement of the world, there were plenty of lunch counters and voting booths that needed attention right here at home.

Yet, for reasons that can only be conjectured, Norman Rockwell wanted a black American included in the picture of hope he would paint as "The Peace Corps." So, again, he went looking for a black model. And again, the Gunns of Stockbridge were of assistance.

When David Gunn, Sr. (Rockwell's pipe-smoking buddy) mentioned to his wife, Florence, that the illustrator was looking for a young black female model, she immediately thought of Loretta Bowens. Loretta was the sixteen year old daughter of Mattie Marena Bowens, one of Florence's closest friends.

In a brief telephone interview, Loretta ruefully acknowledged that she did not remember much about her modeling session with Norman Rockwell. "I was a typical sixteen year old, I guess. My mind was on other things."

Loretta's mother drove them the short ride from their home in Great Barrington to Norman Rockwell's studio in Stockbridge. Loretta was dressed (as were all the young people in the painting) in her collegiate best, right down to the pearl earrings. Her hair was styled to a "T" and her beautiful caramel apple-colored cheeks glowed.

Loretta Bowens recalls that, when she met Norman Rockwell, he looked very stooped over and thin. There was no offer of Coca Cola, and Loretta does not recall receiving a check. Although she doesn't remember much about the photo shoot that, she knows, she *would* remember.

Now an assistant director of case managers for a private social services agency in the Hudson Valley, Loretta Bowens says she had no idea of the importance of "The Peace Corps" painting or of her face in it until she was much older. Only when others started to ask if that was Loretta in the Norman Rockwell painting on the cover of *Look* did she begin to realize how significant it was.

Bowens contacted the Norman Rockwell Museum and was invited to attend a models' reunion in Stockbridge. "It was so exciting," she recalls. "I had no idea that this, that I, was such a big deal. I bought a book and had it signed by some of the other models. I really enjoyed it." I told Loretta that another models' reunion was scheduled at the museum in a few weeks. I asked if she would be going. She hadn't been invited, she replied. Maybe she would call them.

More Modeling the '60's

From the altruism of the Kennedy Peace Corps, Norman Rockwell moved to the utopianism of America's burgeoning suburbs. "New Kids in the Neighborhood" was the artist's next statement about equality, and his next use of models of color.

The May 16th, 1967 issue of *Look* magazine was billed as "A Report on Suburbia" with the added tagline, "The Good Life In Our Exploding Utopia." *Look's* cover for that edition lists the line up of suburban-related stories: "Parties and Prejudices," "Morals and Divorce," "Teenagers in Trouble," and a story entitled "Negro in the Suburbs."

Mrs. Jacqueline Robbins, a young black housewife living in the then all-white Chicago suburb of Park Forest, Illinois with her chemist husband and two sons, reported: "Being a Negro in the middle of white people is like being alone in the middle of a crowd." In Chicago during 1966, the story explained, 179 Negro families moved into white suburbs, more than twice as many as in the previous year, seven times as many as in 1963. "Although Negroes are still a rarity in the green reaches of suburbia," the *Look* article continues, "they are emerging from nearly all the large metropolitan ghettos with increasing frequency." Norman Rockwell's "New Kids in the Neighborhood" ran as a two-page centerfold in this issue, right in the middle of the "Negro in The Suburbs" article.

"New Kids in the Neighborhood" focuses on moving in day for a black family newly-arrived in a fictional white suburb. Norman Rockwell uses black and white children as the focal point of the scene.

Two sets of children are standing in front of a moving van, sizing one another up, while a less-than-friendly face peers at them through the curtains in the house next door. The three white kids, two boys and a girl, are from the neighborhood. The two black kids, presumably brother and sister, were modeled by two of David Gunn, Sr.'s grandchildren: Wray Gunn, Jr. and his cousin Tracy Gunn, Anita's little sister.

Almost stereotypical Rockwell Americana abounds: the boys have baseball gloves, the girls wear hair ribbons and both groups have a pet. The point is made: regardless of the tensions some of the adults may feel, kids are kids.

Children, in any case, are usually not the source of the problem. As Ruby Bridges has remarked, "None of us knows anything about disliking one another when we come into the world. It is something that is passed on to us." Norman Rockwell sought to portray this truth in his illustrations for a children's book about school integration: *Dead End School.*

ᔓ

Dead End School, published in 1968, was written by child psychiatrist Robert Coles and illustrated by Norman Rockwell. Coles had served as therapist to the black children who integrated the New Orleans schools (including Ruby Bridges), then moved to Boston to work with his close friend and colleague, Erik Erickson at Harvard. It was on the basis of their mutual friendship with Erickson that Coles pursued Rockwell's collaboration on *Dead End School.*

In his first letter dated March 7, 1967, Coles states that he is asking Rockwell to illustrate his book because he was "quite moved by that portrait" (referring to "The Problem We All Live With"). "The publishers say that to their knowledge you don't illustrate children's books, and I replied to them that child psychiatrists like me don't usually write children's books. I thought that the two of us might make a very unorthodox but perhaps valuable pair of collaborators." Robert Coles and Norman Rockwell ultimately became not just collaborators, but friends.

Dead End School is the story of two sixth graders, Jim and Larry (they are both black but the narrative never specifically says so), close friends who are separated when a busing program takes one of them to a white school far from their home neighborhood. All of the main characters in the book are black, and Norman Rockwell and Robert Coles agreed that they must be illustrated with "dignity, worldliness and intelligence".

"I've deliberately kept from using the words 'Negro' and 'white'" wrote Coles to Rockwell in a letter dated March 19, 1967, "though clearly the children will be recognized as colored, and *your sensitive grasp of colored children, in my opinion, would really seal the worth and effectiveness of the book* (emphasis mine). I have a feeling that the book would be something really helpful to children all over the country, of both races, and that it could reach them quietly and perhaps lastingly."

According to photographs in the Norman Rockwell Museum and Archives, the modeling session for *Dead End School* took place at Norman Rockwell's studio in Stockbridge with Robert Cole in attendance. Interpretation of the few notes available regarding the session suggests that the two black sixth graders were modeled by a John Halpin and a Ronald Black or Ronald Moody. So far, I have not been able to learn any definitive information regarding where these boys were from, or where they are now.

The remaining three black models, however, were from Pittsfield, Massachusetts. The Reverend Isaiah Jenkins of the Second Congregational Church in Pittsfield, as well as Nancy Hall, a school teacher, modeled as civil rights protestors. The model for the praying mother may have been a Mrs. Pinky Brooks. Unfortunately, that's all I've been able to learn about these models at this time.

Given the "worth and effectiveness" of its topic and the star quality of its creators (Rockwell and Cole) it is peculiar how little documentation, information or analysis exists for *Dead End School.* As far as I can tell, its Norman Rockwell sketches have never been reproduced or critiqued in any other volume. The book itself is out of print.

Even more bizarre, the entry for *Dead End School* on Amazon does not list Norman Rockwell as the illustrator. In fact, a Google search of *Dead End School* resulted in only one site, a rare bookseller that does cite Rockwell. And while the book can be purchased on Amazon for nineteen cents, the exact same edition on the rare book site, the site that lists Norman Rockwell as the illustrator, is priced at seventy dollars.

Richard Reeves, in an article published in the New York Times Magazine in February of 1971, has succinctly noted: "The power of the Rockwell brand." Yet not powerful enough, apparently, to keep a book full of Norman Rockwell drawings of black models from fading away in plain sight.

Nevertheless, 1968 was a good year for Robert Cole and Norman Rockwell as they successfully published the culmination of their joint efforts. 1968 was not, however, such a good year for The United States.

ᔓ

For the United States, 1968 was a terrible year. MLK was assassinated. RFK was assassinated. Then, in November, 1968, Richard Nixon was elected.

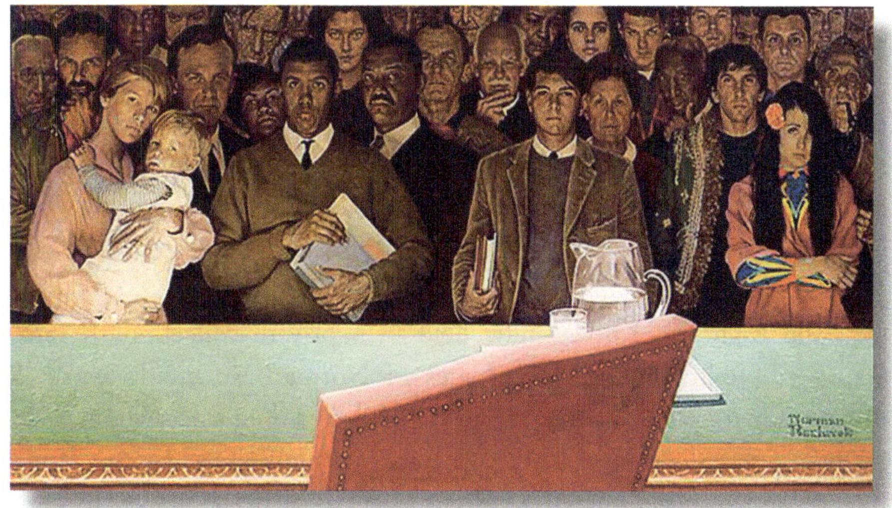

***The Right To Know* by Norman Rockwell. August 20, 1968**

Norman Rockwell's "The Right To Know" appeared in *Look* magazine on August 20, 1968, during the heat of the presidential campaign. Rockwell spent two months working on the illustration, striving to visualize "the information gap that existed between government and the public."

In the painting, a crowd of citizens, black and white, young and old, glares up at an empty chair behind a judge's dais. Some of the models are collegiate and suited up. But in "The Right To Know," as opposed to "The Peace Corps," there are also long hairs and hippies. The title of the accompanying editorial begins, "We are the governed, but we govern too."

The black models in the painting represent three generations of Gunns. To the right, the gray-haired black man is David Gunn, Sr., standing two figures over from a pipe-smoking Norman Rockwell. The middle-aged black man in the center of the painting is David Gunn, Jr., and the black collegiate front and center in the picture is his nephew, St. Clair Gunn,

Jr. The tiny black woman glaring over St. Clair's shoulder is Velma Gunn, David Gunn, Jr.'s wife.

In Norman Rockwell's United Nations mural the people appeal to government leaders. In his "Golden Rule," they ignore government leaders. In "The Right To Know," Norman Rockwell's people seem to be indicting government leaders. Part of the *Look* editorial reads:

"And listen to us, you who lead, for we are listening harder for truth that you have not always offered us. Your voice must be ours, and ours speaks of cities that are not safe, and of wars we do not want, of poor in a land of plenty, and of a world that will not take the shape our arms would give it."

"The Right To Know," now held in a private collection, is rarely displayed publicly. Most anthologies of Norman Rockwell's work do not include it. Ironically, very few Rockwell fans even know about it. It's intriguing to consider: what if black Rockwell model David Gunn, Jr., in his suit and tie, were just as widely recognized as black Rockwell model Paul Adams, shirtless with his prayer bowl?

∽

As the tumultuous 1960's drew to a close, Norman Rockwell was not sure what the 1968 theme would be for his illustrations for the Boy Scout calendar. But of one thing he was sure: given the liberating ride of the sixties, it was time for the Boy Scouts to get colored.

Chapter 7

COLORING THE BOY SCOUTS

". . . that God damned calendar."
Norman Rockwell

In *The Saturday Evening Post* article entitled, "Rockwell's Real People," Ernie Hall, Stockbridge native and Rockwell model declares: "Remember all those Boy Scout calendars he (Rockwell) did for years? He did those for nothing." It seems that even the "real people" in Rockwell's world were unaware of the famous illustrator's true feelings about the Boy Scouts of America.

Since 1924, Norman Rockwell had been paid $5,000 for each Boy Scout Christmas calendar cover he created; one painting, every year. And every year, he enjoyed doing that painting less and less.

Finally, in June of 1957, Rockwell realized it was time to start "that God damned calendar" again and he realized he'd had it. The artist called the Boy Scout National Office to resign his commission. But they offered to double his pay if he would stay: from $5000 to $10,000 for one painting, every year.

ꕥ

Every June, while Norman Rockwell sweated over what to do about the Boy Scout calendar, towns all over America were gearing up for their Independence Day parades. And the 4th of July parade in Pittsfield, Massachusetts was always a doozy: Alfred Persip, commander of Pittsfield's American Legion Post #68, saw to it.

There is nothing as all-American as a parade. And there was nobody more all-American than Alfred K. Persip, Sr. His family had been respected people of color in western Massachusetts since the early 1800's. In 1863, Alfred's maternal grandfather, Charles Hamilton, traveling to Boston from his Berkshire mountains home, had been among the first to join "The Glory Regiment," Colonel Robert Shaw's famed 54th Massachusetts Volunteer Infantry of colored soldiers.

Alfred Persip followed in his grandfather's footsteps, literally and figuratively. In 1916, Persip mounted the steps of the Pittsfield City Hall, presenting himself to recruiters as ready to sign on with the other Pittsfield boys going overseas to battle the Bosch. But the recruiters wouldn't take him: colored men were not wanted among the Pittsfield enlisted contingent.

Undeterred, Alfred traveled fifty miles south to Springfield where he finally convinced an Army recruiter to take him. Thus, Alfred Persip, Sr. became the first man from Pittsfield's large and historic colored community to enlist to fight in WWI.

The young recruit was assigned to the 372nd Colored Infantry Regiment, fighting under the direction of French officers: American officers refused to lead colored troops. The 372nd went on to distinguish itself throughout the European theatre, so much so that its men were awarded the *Croix de Guerre* with palm leaves, France's highest military honor.

ঌ

On a balmy June Sunday morning in 1946, forty-seven year old Alfred Persip still manifested soldierly bearing as he stood in the living room of his home, waiting for the rest of his family so they could head out to service at the First Baptist Church of Pittsfield. Persip was studying the plans for the 4th of July parade. As usual, the members of American Legion Post #68 would kick it off with the World War 1 vets, including Alfred, at the lead. The high school band would follow, then Boy Scout Troop 47.

Persip enjoyed working with the Scouts. A certified horticulturalist, he met often with the troop at its meeting place in the Epworth Mission, teaching the boys the skills required for their horticulture as well as for their woodworking badges. However, neither of Alfred's sons, Little Al nor Richard, had been Scouts. The all-white troop was not quite ready for that yet.

But Big Al Persip's unflinching belief in America also led him to be an optimist about the Boy Scouts. One day the Scouts would be ready. One day, he might even have a grandson in Troop 47.

ര

Norman Rockwell, however, had no such optimism about the Boy Scouts of America. For Rockwell, the Boy Scouts were a pain in the neck. Increasingly, the famous illustrator found scouting topics dull, flat and uninteresting. Ironically, these were the very same barbs being used by some New York art critics to describe *his* work.

Trout fishing buddy, Arlington neighbor and fellow illustrator John Atherton couldn't understand why Norman felt compelled to keep producing that "propaganda, sentimental trash." The answer, very simply, was the money. The Boy Scouts of America paid very, very well. With three sons in prep school and college and a wife receiving intensive, exclusive and expensive psychiatric care, Norman Rockwell needed that money.

Over the years, however, correspondence between Rockwell and Scout officials grew increasingly testy. The illustrator was annoyed by the bureaucrats' nit-picking corrections of badge placement and rope knots in the draft paintings he sent them. High-level Scout officials badgered him constantly for corporate endorsements and personal favors. But what really got in Norman Rockwell's craw was the organization's injunction against including colored Scouts on the calendar.

The Boy Scouts of America "are simply going to have to devise some new good deeds or Brown and Bigelow (the calendar's publisher) will be in a hell of a fix," Rockwell griped to an interviewer in 1945. But nothing changed. The artist soldiered on with his lucrative albatross for twenty-three more years.

Then, in 1968 (the same year he painted "The Right To Know"), Norman Rockwell decided to take matters into his own hands. If the Boy Scouts of America couldn't come up with some new, significant and relevant good deeds, then Rockwell would initiate a new good deed for them. Ready or not, the Boy Scouts were going to get some color in their calendar.

The illustrator was not sure what the theme of the 1968 calendar would be. However, one concept kept playing around in his head: scouts in a marching band, playing various musical instruments. Norman Rockwell grabbed a sheet of paper and scribbled down the names of boys in the Stockbridge area who might be right as models for the band: Greg Pering, Bryan Wood, Hank Bergmans. He would need to find a fat boy and a boy with glasses. And Rockwell wanted to find a colored boy. A colored boy scout to be exact, the band member who, the artist visualized, would be the one playing the cymbals.

Rockwell recalled that his friend, Dale Lock, was a Boy Scout leader. Lock was pastor of the First Baptist Church in Pittsfield, Massachusetts. Established in 1823, First Baptist was the city's first fully integrated house of worship.

Reverend Lock had mentioned to Rockwell that the Boy Scout troop he led, Scout Troop 47, was now integrated, as well: two Negro boys were now members. Rockwell asked his friend to get in touch with the parents of these boys and ask them to let their sons model for him. One of the boys was Isaac A. Crawford, III. His mother's name was Rosemary, nee Persip.

Rosemary Persip Crawford belongs to that Black Brahmin group (as do the Gunns of Stockbridge and the Adams clan in Washington County) of families who trace their roots in their respective communities back to the 1700's. A small park in Pittsfield is named after her father, that inveterate patriot and parade organizer, "Big Al" Persip. Rosemary Persip Crawford would meet the DAR's qualifications in a heartbeat.

Rosemary's husband, Isaac Crawford, Jr., came from an equally illustrious lineage. He was a former student at Tuskegee Institute and a Navy veteran. His grandparents had founded the historic Macedonia Baptist Church in Great Barrington, Massachusetts, the first black church in the area. In his memoir, *Beating the Odds: A Story of Survival,* Isaac Crawford, Jr. traces the Crawford family line back to 1834. Black Boy Scout Isaac A. Crawford, III came from an illustrious all-American background, indeed.

When Rosemary Crawford was told by Doris Lock, Reverend Lock's wife, that Norman Rockwell wanted her son Isaac to model for him, she excitedly gave her approval. Rockwell had offered to pay Isaac III the standard modeling fee: ten dollars for the session. The famous illustrator asked that Isaac wear his Scout uniform for the photo shoot. Doris volunteered that she and Reverend Locke would be happy to drive Isaac over to Stockbridge for the session.

When twelve year old Isaac Crawford, Scout uniform crisply pressed, Scout cap jauntily cocked, was ushered into Rockwell's Stockbridge studio, he looked just as sharp and impressive as his granddad Alfred Persip had leading a 4th of July parade.

A seventy-four year old Norman Rockwell greeted the youngster with a warm smile and a cold Coke. The artist joked and smiled and coached Isaac as he maneuvered the cymbals and Louie Lamore, Rockwell's photographer, snapped the poses. Although Isaac remembers Lamore as being a bit snappish, overall a good time was had by all. "Rockwell was very gracious," Isaac Crawford recalls. "Being in his studio, I was in awe."

But Rockwell did not use Isaac's photos or the marching band theme for the 1968 Boy Scout calendar. Instead, he submitted "Scouting is An Outing," prominently portraying another colored scout, Chancey Stockton of Troop 52 in Troy, New York, running along in the midst of the enthusiastic troop.

Norman Rockwell did, however, use the marching band concept for a special Bicentennial Boy Scout calendar published in the spring of 1976. It was Norman Rockwell's last work for the Boy Scouts. Although most of the models for this calendar came from a photo session Rockwell held at his studio in November of 1973, there, stepping along with the troop, marches a colored Boy Scout: Isaac Crawford.

Alfred Persip's dream had come true: his grandson was a Boy Scout. And not just any Boy Scout. Isaac Persip Crawford, III, was a *Norman Rockwell* Boy Scout. How American a story was that?

Well, maybe in some ways, *too* American. Norman Rockwell included black Scouts in each of his Scout calendars from 1970 until his last work in 1976. When Joseph Csatari, Rockwell's protégé and assistant, succeeded Rockwell as official Boy Scout artist in 1977, he wrote, in a handwritten letter to the artist, that he "had hopes of carrying on the Norman Rockwell tradition." However, when Csatari sought to honor Rockwell with the 2009 calendar, "Scouting Salutes," not one person of color, Scout or otherwise, appears in the picture.

This fact is particularly disturbing since Csatari describes "Scouting Salutes" as modeled on Norman Rockwell's 1968 piece, "Scouting Is An Outing"–the piece in which the determined artist had boldly integrated the calendar with black Boy Scout Chancey Stockton. It's as if Rockwell had painted the black Scouts in, and then they were airbrushed back out again.

ꟹ

Rockwell model Isaac Crawford, III is now a leading fashion apparel executive and the CEO of Wahconah Group. His company recently launched the *Rain, Heat and Snow* brand of apparel and accessories for the United States Post Office. Urbane, accomplished and confident, Crawford shook his head in rueful recognition when I told him the story of the 2009 calendar. He was not surprised. "When I came back and told people that I was a Rockwell model, that I had just modeled for the Boy Scout calendar, nobody believed me. They still don't."

Chapter 8

THE NAVAJOS, THE ILLUSTRATOR, AND GLEN CANYON DAM

"Glen Canyon Dam sits on the Navajo Reservation, but its proponents were, and its primary beneficiaries remain, non-Indian people."
Sherry L. Smith and Brian Frehner, authors of "Indians & Energy"

"Get me a Navajo family."
Norman Rockwell

Controversy with the Boy Scouts of America or anybody else for that matter was far from Norman Rockwell's mind in December of 1946. Rockwell was on vacation, rolling luxuriously across Indian lands on "The Super Chief," pride of the Santa Fe Railway.

"The Chief," as it was fondly referred to, began its run in Chicago. The train traveled through Illinois, Missouri, Kansas, Colorado, New Mexico and Arizona at speeds often reaching 100 mph as it barreled towards its terminus, Union Station in Los Angeles.

From the comfort of domed viewing cars, passengers on "The Chief" could marvel at the curving canyons of New Mexico and Arizona as the train threaded chasms barely a few feet wider than itself. The Pullmans roared past spectacular landscapes and pristine vistas not visible from Route 66 ("America's Main Street" as author Rick Antonsen would later refer to it), famous for the cross-country automobile trips of the less well-heeled.

The elegant traveled on "The Super Chief." Movie stars and celebrities made up its clientele. Among the train's dignitaries in December, 1946 was Norman Rockwell and family.

ᔓ

The entire Rockwell family–Norman, Mary and their three sons Jarvis, Thomas and Peter–were traveling to Alhambra, California, a suburb of Los Angeles, to spend the holidays with Mary's parents, the Barstows. Norman was actually considering staying on in California for a few months after Mary and the boys went back to Vermont.

Over the last several years, Rockwell had taken several extended retreats to the home of his California in-laws. Ostensibly for the sake of his health, Rockwell in fact appreciated getting away from Vermont winters and from the chaotic cacophony that his house sometimes became, what with Mary and the three boys shut in because of the weather.

Rockwell also loved indulging his ego in the southern California limelight, playing the part of celebrity illustrator with the Hollywood set. He rented a studio while he was on the coast, keeping up his prodigious daily schedule of work. It was during these West coast sojourns, for example, that Rockwell created extensive advertising images for *Twentieth Century Fox.* In 1946, Norman Rockwell was at the height of his national prominence and the movie moguls, along with most of middle-brow America, loved him.

ᔓ

The Super Chief slowly picked up speed as it pulled out of the station in Winslow, Arizona. "La Posada," the last Harvey House built by the chain, disappeared around the bend as the powerful locomotive pulled its cars westward. Speeding towards Flagstaff, passengers looking north were rewarded with vistas of Coconino National Forest, Gray Mountain and the Colorado River flowing through magnificent Glen Canyon, 140 miles away. Gazing out the train's window, a vacationing Norman Rockwell could not have known that, twenty-two years later, he would return to this landscape with a different wife for a different, more serious purpose–and that Glen Canyon would be gone.

ᔓ

For thousands of years, the Colorado River flowed freely through Glen Canyon. "The Cathedral in the Desert," "Music Temple," and "Gregory Natural Bridge" were but three of the many magical monuments that soared up among the canyon's ridges and escarpments.

Navajo Indians lived here and considered these places sacred. Anglo residents, such as river runner Ken Sleight (immortalized as the rascally environmentalist "Seldom Seen Smith" in Edward Abbey's anarchist primer, *The Monkey Wrench Gang*) also revered the canyon and made their living from it. When the Rockwell family rode through in 1946, the region had no Lake Powell and no Page, Arizona. In 1946, there was no Glen Canyon Dam.

ᔓ

Construction of Glen Canyon Dam began on October 15, 1956. President Eisenhower set off the massive federal project's first blast of dynamite by remote control from the White House. The dam was designed to hold back the waters of the Colorado River, filling Glen Canyon and creating Lake Powell, a reservoir named after John Wesley Powell, an early Colorado River explorer.

One of the largest reclamation projects in United States history, the dam would house the seventh largest hydro-electric power plant in the world, scheduled to generate up to 900,000 kilowatts of electricity. Anglo engineers, contractors and laborers from all over the United States swarmed to the site, attracted by good jobs at good government wages. They set up a ramshackle settlement on the lip of Glen Canyon that morphed into the town of Page, Arizona, later dubbed "the town the dam built."

The Indians who had lived in the area withdrew to native communities farther east and south. One of those communities was Black Mesa, Arizona.

Black Mesa was a small, traditional Navajo compound, built around its chapter house and community school. The little village sat about 60 miles southeast of the growing white settlement of Page. When construction began on Glen Canyon Dam in 1956, the Navajo John Lane took whatever odd jobs he could get on the project. But his home was back in Black Mesa.

There he built a *hogan* (the traditional Navajo shelter), married, and started a family.

As Lane went about establishing his life on the reservation, it is highly unlikely that any Rockwell illustrations hung on the walls of his home. But in thirteen years, Norman Rockwell would be a guest at the hogan of John Lane. And the John Lane family would become Norman Rockwell models.

ᔓᔕ

The Blue Room, *my father's pool hall and backroom gambling emporium, was 2,293 miles from Black Mesa, Arizona. But in 1956, Indians were among its most loyal patrons.*

Located, literally, across the railroad tracks that bisected Bridgeport, Connecticut, the Blue Room, *along with its neighbors the* Elks Club *and* Mamie's Restaurant *formed the heart of the colored part of town. These establishments were the go-to destinations for colored men looking to spend some of their good factory and construction job paychecks on a little R&R. Indians were sometimes among this group, Native American ironworkers up from erecting skyscrapers and bridges in New York City, 50 miles and a one hour train ride to the south.*

One of my father's favorite mantras was, "The only thing that's real is real estate." And Buddy Allen was building his fortune, one piece of property at a time. He was buying that property with the earnings from the Blue Room, *both its front and back room activities. Excellent businessman that he was, when a customer couldn't meet a bet, Buddy was happy to serve as pawn broker, holding watches, cuff links, even wedding rings as collateral until the player could make good.*

So when, on a warm July evening in 1956, Lady Luck failed to smile upon one of the Indian poker players, and the hapless man, to cover his losses, offered my father deeds to two plots of land in Burnt Water, Arizona, Buddy Allen was happy to oblige.

ᔓᔕ

Glen Canyon Dam was officially opened and dedicated with great fanfare by First Lady Ladybird Johnson on the 22nd of September, 1966.

By 1968, however, it was clear that Glen Canyon Dam was becoming a public relations disaster.

Ken Sleight proclaimed that the dam had buried the heart of canyon country: "When they flooded Glen Canyon, they killed all those things I loved." David Brower, the Sierra Club's first executive director, called the dam "America's most regretted environmental mistake." Even "Mr. Conservative," former senator Barry Goldwater, admitted that he was sorry he had voted for the project. Criticism was rampant.

The Bureau of Reclamation, the federal agency responsible for the project, searched for a tactic, a strategy to transform the image of all of its water reclamation projects into a positive one. And so in 1969 the Bureau, universally known for its engineering accomplishments, decided to promote its accomplishments through art.

Forty of America's most prominent artists were commissioned to visit and tour the reclamation projects throughout the West, at government expense. In exchange, they were requested to capture their impressions on canvas and to donate their paintings to the Bureau of Reclamation. Under the leadership of John DeWitt, a Washington-based director at the Bureau, and with the on-site supervision of Will Rusho, Public Affairs Officer for the Bureau in Arizona, the painters had free hand to depict any subject they chose as long as it pertained to a water resources reclamation program in the West.

In the end, over 300 pieces of art were created. Anton Refregier, for example, painted construction scenes at Grand Coulee Dam. Richard Diebenkorn depicted the irrigation fields along the lower Colorado River. And Norman Rockwell captured the troubling message of Glen Canyon Dam.

❧

Although trained and hired by the Bureau of Reclamation as an engineer, Will Rusho became, over time, more and more of a historian of the areas affected by the water reclamation projects, especially the areas in and around Glen Canyon. "So I would ask the photographers to take pictures of these side things," Rusho recollected. On one occasion, his boss caught him at it. "Your job is to be concerned with that hunk of concrete down there and nothing else," Rusho recalled being told. "But," he continued, "I tended to ignore him."

Thus it was that when Will Rusho was asked to introduce the artist Norman Rockwell to a reclamation project, he took the famous illustrator to Glen Canyon Dam.

ɞ

On a drizzly October 19, 1969, Rockwell arrived in Page, Arizona with his third wife, Molly and with John DeWitt, a Bureau of Land Reclamation Director who had traveled out from Washington to be a part of the famous illustrator's entourage. Will Rusho served as the local tour guide. Their first stop was the emerging Lake Powell. After touring the Lake, the group went on to the dam construction site where DeWitt wanted Rockwell to start making sketches. According to Rusho, Rockwell looked at the dam and said, "That's a mechanical drawing. To do something like that, where's some human interest?"

Rusho, the amateur historian-cum-engineer, remarked that Navajos lived in the area. "Well get me a Navajo family," Rockwell replied.

Rockwell wanted to paint people, not rocks. He had set up his first studio in Stockbridge with its large plate-glass window overlooking Main Street precisely because he had wanted to see "people instead of mountains." You could take the boy out of New York City, but you couldn't take New York City out of the boy.

So Will Rusho, Norman, Molly and John DeWitt all piled back into the car. Driving southeast out of Page on Rte. 98, heading towards Black Mesa, they were looking for Navajos.

Finally, after driving in the rain for some while, they spotted a *hogan*. Rusho got out of the car and approached the home as a Navajo man emerged from inside. "I don't speak English. Don't speak English!" the stern faced fellow declared. The government official paused a moment, then quipped, "Too bad. I've got an artist out in the car that would like to sketch you doing something." Then he added, "It's Norman Rockwell."

"Norman Rockwell!" John Lane exclaimed. "I'll be right back." Lane rushed back into the *hogan*, after a few minutes re-emerging with his wife (who was carrying an infant), his little daughter and his son. The family dog meekly slunk around the corner, joining the gathering.

Introductions were made all around. Then the group went down to the stable and led out the family horse. Rockwell arranged various tableaus of the family as Molly snapped slide after colored slide. Rusho snapped several black and white photos of the Lanes, as well.

As Rockwell visited with the Lane family at their *hogan* near Black Mesa, a concept for the commemorative painting solidified in the illustrator's mind. After the models were paid, and warm farewells were made, the artist's entourage headed back up Rte. 98, back to Glen Canyon Dam. There, Rockwell asked Rusho to snap photos of him, standing on the canyon rim, looking over at the dam.

Will Rusho remembers Norman Rockwell as "so accommodating, so nice," full of "nothing but compliments and thanks for our help." All involved thought it was a very inspiring and worthwhile trip.

∽

Rockwell was indeed inspired. But unfortunately for the Bureau of Reclamation, not in the way that they had intended. Will Rusho wryly observes, "Then, when we get the painting, he has combined the two. He has put the family and the horse and the dog standing on the canyon rim, looking at the dam. And that is the famous painting that we have. "

"Glen Canyon Dam", a "51" x 77" oil on canvas, was completed by Norman Rockwell when he returned to his Stockbridge studio. The Bureau paid Rockwell for the painting, but it was not pleased. In the rigid back of John Lane, the drooping shoulders of his son, the fixed glare of his wife, even in the bewildered expression of the dog, Rockwell painted not only the dam, but more significantly, the Indians' condemning reaction to it.

Laura Claridge, Rockwell biographer, observes, "The finished oil, with a sad, dignified. . . Indian family occupying the foreground of the otherwise impersonal industrial vista, appears almost subversively at odds with the commission Rockwell had been given."

Hiding The Canyon

The Bureau of Reclamation deep-sixed "Glen Canyon Dam," the painting. The illustration does not appear in most compilations of Norman Rockwell's works, and most Rockwell fans have neither heard of nor seen it. The original painting hangs, somewhat ironically, in the Glen Canyon Dam Museum at Page, Arizona.

Since 2000, Lake Powell has been drying up. In fact, parts of "The Cathedral in The Desert" are now visible. Some say, prophetically, that the town of Page may be drying up, as well. Glen Canyon may be coming back.

From the time I was about ten years old, I recall my father occasionally stating, "I own property in Arizona, you know. One day I'm going to go out there and see it." My little sister and I would dutifully nod our heads and say, "Yes, Daddy" while shooting glances at each other and doing mental eye rolls. (To do an actual eye roll in front of our father would have occurred to us just about as often as swallowing worms.)

By the time I got into my forties, however, and was helping my father manage his business affairs, I knew that Daddy hadn't made it up. I'd seen the deeds: Buddy Allen did own two lots of land in a place officially called Sanders, Arizona, but known to the Navajos who lived on the reservation lands around it as Burnt Water.

My dad had never seen his land, and he had never flown on an airplane. So, for his 70th birthday, using my cache of frequent flyer points, I took us out to the high desert crossroads of Sanders, Arizona. Daddy's lots were vacant, thank goodness: no squatters. But just about everything in and around Sanders was vacant. I remember being mesmerized by the tumbleweed blowing across Route 191, the main and only road through town. My father was mesmerized by the whole experience. It was his land, and it was beautiful.

My dad chatted up the white postmistress (the post office being the only government building in the community) about what he saw as the glowing prospects for development in Sanders. Then we strolled down the street to the local eatery.

Perching ourselves on counter stools in the empty cafe, my father and I turned our brightest smiles on the Navajo woman who approached us with menus. "Ya'at'eeh" *I ventured, visualizing the syllables from my Conversational Navajo Dictionary. "Hello, I'm Buddy Allen from Bridgeport, Connecticut and this is my daughter, Lady Jane," my father offered, extending a wrinkled but still very strong black hand. "She brought me out here to see my land."*

The waitress returned the handshake and looked into his face, smiling slightly. "You have land here?" she asked softly. "Oh oh", I thought. "Yes," my father replied. "I've owned it thirty years and never seen it."

Our coffee and fry bread arrived, and my dad and I sat and ate in that comfortable quiet we had come to expect and respect in Native American places. The waitress moved up and down behind the counter, cleaning this and that while we slowly sipped and chewed. There was no chatter.

I was contemplating getting another order of fry bread when the bell over the café door jangled and a Navajo teenager entered, followed by an old Navajo man walking with a cane. The old man waited by a table while the young man approached me. "Hello," he began. "Are you the lady who brought her father here to see his land?" "Ah, yes. Yes I am," I replied, wondering how he had found this out. As far as I could tell, the waitress had never left the counter, and there didn't seem to be a telephone out front.

"My grandfather heard that there was a man here who came from all the way back East to see his land, and that his daughter brought him out here to see it. My grandfather would like to meet you. He's an elder here."

The boy had barely finished his last words when my father was off the café stool and across the room, hand outstretched to the elderly Indian. "How do you do? My name is Buddy Allen, from Bridgeport, Connecticut. And this is my daughter, Lady Jane." The young man translated the introductions into Navajo (I think I got the "Lady Jane" part). Then the two old men, Navajo and black, sat down to a two-hour conversation.

As the waitress poured more coffee and the grandson translated, the elders explored the vicissitudes of family and how young people just didn't get it: that the only thing that was real was real estate. They compared war stories, agreeing that a colored man, black or red, had to hold onto his land for dear life, because the white man had no regard for the colored man or for his land. Because the white man, without a thought, would just disregard the man and savage the land, the way he had done 200 miles north, up Route 191, at Glen Canyon Dam.

ര

Rena Babbitt Lane still lives in a *hogan* on the Black Mesa reservation, and she still only speaks Navajo. She is 92 years old and the widow of John Lane.

Rena is one of the founders of Black Mesa Weavers. That's how I found her–through their website. The organization's Anglo director put me in touch with Rena's English-speaking granddaughter, Jolinda Miller Hawkins. Apparently, until I contacted them, no one in Black Mesa had ever seen or heard of Norman Rockwell's painting, "Glen Canyon Dam."

After an intense exchange of phone calls, emails and .jpegs, Jolinda concluded that her grandparents were not the John Lanes in the Rockwell painting. But she thinks they may be the family of her grandfather's cousin.

The names "John" and "Juhn" are common among the Navajo. From what has been pieced together thus far, Rena's husband, Juhn Lane, was first cousin to the John Lane family that posed for Norman Rockwell. Jolinda and I, therefore, are on a mission: working the exigencies of dead cell phones, washed out roads and other realities of communication on the reservation, we are trying to circulate photos of the "Glen Canyon Dam" models among the Navajo nation. The little boy in the painting, and the little girl and baby in the photos taken by Will Rusho and Molly Rockwell, may very well still be alive.

But if so, why haven't they talked about their memorable experience? Why doesn't anyone know their story? Well, for one thing, it is not "Navajo" to talk about oneself, and certainly not to brag.

But also, maybe, like other Rockwell models of color, the John Lane family once did talk of that special visit ("Norman Rockwell showed up one day at our *hogan*!") only to be met with disbelief and ridicule. Nobody ever connects the Indian features of the John Lane family with Norman Rockwell's people. (The children in the photos may even think that those childhood memories were ones that they had made up.)

Rockwell sought them out and placed them front and center in one of his major works. That is where he wanted them to be. But somehow, these Navajo models, like so many other Norman Rockwell models of color, faded into the background, became "hidden in plain sight."

ᔓ

I inherited and still own those two lots in Burnt Water aka *Sanders, Arizona. Just ninety miles west of Winslow (the Winslow of* Eagles *fame) I hope to go back there soon and take it easy myself. Eat some fry bread, listen to the wind, meet up with some Lanes. Get out the trusty Navajo dictionary.* Ya'at'eeh.

Chapter 9

NORMAN ROCKWELL SAVED MY LIFE

"Norman Rockwell saved my life. Do you see, do you see, do you see, do you see, do you see? All I had was a magazine ad. Norman Rockwell saved my life."
Jim Wann, composer/songwriter

"I just wanted to do something important." A frustrated Norman Rockwell nursed this sentiment throughout his adult life. What the troubled illustrator did not know was that he *was* doing something critically important: his work was motivating and instructing thousands of young black art students all over America.

I met and interviewed members of this little-known Rockwell legacy when I visited several museums around the country that were hosting Norman Rockwell shows. For example, at The Brooklyn Museum of Art, I encountered Robin Jordan. She was there savoring Ron Schick's show, "Behind The Camera," a compendium of the photographs used by Norman Rockwell to create his illustrations.

I introduced myself to Jordan as a writer who was researching a book about Norman Rockwell and people of color. Then I asked her why she had come to see the exhibit.

Robin Jordan, a mature woman, short and wiry with cocoa brown skin and lively eyes, informed me that she had visited the show every day since it had opened. Now a retired fashion illustrator, she confided to me that while growing up, she had two heroes: Jackie Robinson and Norman Rockwell. I offered her a coffee in the museum café and asked her to tell me her story.

ᔓᔕ

In the winter of 1946, one-year-old Robin Jordan came to live with her Jamaican-American grandparents in their building superintendent's apartment on Eastern Parkway in Brooklyn. Robin's mother could no longer keep her. Her father had never been on the scene.

As soon as she could walk, Robin Jordan trailed behind her grandfather while he made his daily rounds to the utility rooms on each floor of their building. The old man gathered up the rubbish. The little girl collected discarded 10x12 pieces of cardboard, inserts the white, predominantly Jewish tenants of her building had received inside their freshly laundered, pressed and folded shirts.

Soon Robin was using these "easels" to turn out sketch after sketch, using whatever pens, pencils or, when they miraculously appeared, crayons she could lay her hands on.

At seven years' old, Robin Jordan was small and skinny and dark. She could not read well. She could not write well. She could not talk well: she had a severe stutter.

Although her grandmother neatly braided her thick, wooly hair, there wasn't much money for bows. And then there was this: Robin was the only black child in her class, the grandbaby of building superintendents in a school dominated by the sons and daughters of well-to-do strivers. The stress and isolation of her reality only made Robin's learning disorders worse.

By the time she was eleven, Robin was close to suicidal. Drawing was her only language, her only fluent means of communicating with the world. So when, as she was pouring through discarded magazines looking for images to copy, Robin came upon a photo of Norman Rockwell, stating, "We're looking for people who like to draw," she felt the famous artist had thrown her a lifeline.

The Famous Artists' School was founded in 1948 by Norman Rockwell and Albert Dorne, another world-renowned illustrator. Glowingly described in hundreds of newspaper and magazine advertisements, the correspondence school offered enrollees the opportunity to study with and get feedback from Norman Rockwell as well as from eleven other "famous artists."

Initially, each of the founding artists designed his own course. Then, upon enrolling, students had the opportunity to choose the artist whose work they wished to study. Eventually, however, the course curriculums proved to be too advanced for most students. Besides that, everyone wanted to study with Norman Rockwell.

So elements from each artist's course were combined to create a more basic program. The school's founders were intimately involved with the creation of the courses for this program, producing numerous pieces of original art which were reproduced for demonstrations and examples in the texts. Moreover, they also worked closely with the team of instructors who critiqued students' work. Frequent training sessions and workshops for the instructors insured that Rockwell and Dorne's vision was replicated.

Each course consisted of 24 lessons. Tuition at the Westport, Connecticut-based school was $300 a year, paid in $25 monthly installments. Paints and supplies were extra, usually amounting to an additional $11 a month. Given the .40-hour minimum wage in 1948, this path to an artist's career clearly was not for everyone.

But thousands of aspiring illustrators from around the country sought to scrape together the monthly tuition in order to attend the *Famous Artists School.* Some of them, like Robin Jordan, were black.

Robin and her grandparents were able to afford only a few lessons. But she went on copying Rockwell illustrations from the covers of discarded *Saturday Evening Posts*. After a stint in the military, Robin Jordan was able to complete her art studies and secure a career as a fashion illustrator for several New York City department stores. "It all began with a magazine ad, and Norman Rockwell."

ꕤ

Other people of color in The Brooklyn Museum that day were paying tribute to Norman Rockwell, as well. My next self-introduction was to seventeen year old Ladee Shanese Martin, a senior at Charlotte Amalie High School which is located on the American Virgin Island of St. Thomas. A slim, honey-colored young woman with fashion model features, Ladee informed me that she had discovered Norman Rockwell just the year before.

Seeking inspiration as she began her advanced placement art class during the first week of the term, the young artist had come upon a book featuring The Saturday Evening Post covers of Norman Rockwell. These were "realistic paintings," not the abstract spotches that seemed to be the preference of so many of her contemporaries.

Ladee Shanese Martin sat down and read. And then she started to sketch. She drew illustration after illustration, using Norman Rockwell as her guide. "I particularly liked how he portrayed facial expressions," she told me as we attempted not to block the passage of others in the crowded gallery space.

Ladee's art teacher, Susan Edwards, noted the high quality of her star pupil's work. Edwards, a white woman who also served as chair of the art department, described herself on an educators' website as passionate about the role of art in shaping students' lives: "I teach teenagers how to get the most out of their artistic talent and to look at things in a new way". Appreciating the extraordinary quality of Ladee's work, the astute instructor submitted the young student's best piece of class work, "Final Exams," to the 2010 St. Thomas Congressional Art Competition.

The Congressional Art Competition provides members of Congress an opportunity to encourage and recognize the artistic talents of their young constituents. Since 1982, over 650,000 high school students have been involved with the nationwide competition. In the May, 2010 St. Thomas Congressional Art Competition, Ladee Shanese Martin's drawing, "Final Exams," won third place.

A proud Susan Edwards proclaimed on her blog:

> "Last night my student Ladee Martin was recognized at the Virgin Islands Council on the Arts for her amazing drawing, "Final Exam." She received her certificate from Congresswoman Donna Christensen. The first-place winner is from Country Day School on St Croix and her teacher Monica Marin suggested we take our talented seniors to portfolio review day (at Cooper Union) in New York next fall. What an excellent idea!"

Serendipitously, when Ladee Shanese Martin and her teacher/chaperone Susan Edwards traveled to New York, so did Ron Schick's show. Thus, a seventeen year old black girl from the Virgin Islands, at the beginning of her artistic career, and a sixty year old black woman from Brooklyn, at the close of hers, both found themselves in the galleries of the Brooklyn Museum, acknowledging and again studying and again learning from their mutual guide and inspiration, Norman Rockwell.

❧

At Norman Rockwell exhibits in Fort Lauderdale, Florida, Washington, D.C., and Brooklyn, New York, I talked with person after person of color whose education and/or career had been guided and inspired by the work of Norman Rockwell.

Zawadi Kirksey-Lamb, a 19 year old illustration major at The Maryland Institute, College of Art, was exploring the Steven Spielberg and George Lucas collections of Norman Rockwell works on exhibition at The National Portrait Gallery in Washington, D.C. When I asked her why she had come to see the show Zawadi, turning her singular intensity from inspection of a Rockwell sketch to the consideration of my question, responded that she had "always" known she wanted to be an illustrator. "I want to be a painter that tells stories," she said.

Zawadi was a native of New Orleans, and Norman Rockwell illustrations were always in the texts and study books of her Catholic girls' school. Then, when Hurricane Katrina swept through, the Kirksey-Lamb family was forced into a two year exile. It was difficult to get supplies during this time, but Zawadi worked on her sketching as much and as often as she could. The human drama all around her offered unlimited opportunities for "telling stories," And her appreciation of Norman Rockwell's style soared.

"His work is not static," Zawadi Kirksey-Lamb observed, as she indicated to me that she wanted to get back to studying the sketch before her. "Rockwell had the ability to wed photo realism with a life-like quality. And that's what I want to do: realism with life."

In the next gallery, a "traditionally built" black woman was energetically talking with her significantly slimmer male companion as they approached a Rockwell painting of a young woman curled up with a book on an old coach in an attic, the light from a dormer window streaming in from behind her. I smiled as I walked towards the couple, but before I could make my introduction the lady, swathed in bright West African kente cloth, dreadlocks flowing, turned and enveloped me in her arms like a long-lost friend. Our greetings were all warm smiles and croons of, "How ya doin," done only as well-raised black people know how to do it.

An art therapist in the Washington, D.C. public school system, Brenda Nixon and her husband, Mark, a skilled craftsman, had been on their way to the Metro (Washington's rapid rail system) when they saw the sign outside The National Portrait Museum announcing the Rockwell/Lucas/Spielberg show. Neither Brenda nor Mark had ever been in the museum, nor did either of them know anything about Norman Rockwell. But it had started to rain, admission was free, so they had decided to come in.

The first painting they had seen as they had turned into the gallery was that of the girl reading on the couch. And Brenda had been overcome with emotion.

Glancing with relief at my regulation tour guide attire (khaki skirt, white blouse), name badge firmly affixed and an official-looking document dangling from a lanyard around my neck, Brenda assumed I was a museum docent. (I wore my D.C. tour guide license and gear when doing these museum interviews to soften the "fisheyes" of security guards, as I hung out for hours at the exhibits.)

An excited Brenda poured out her questions. Who was that girl in the painting? Was that a Norman Rockwell painting? Who was Norman Rockwell?

After explaining that I was a writer not a docent, I offered that I could still answer some of her questions. The girl in the painting was Jo, one of the main characters in Louise May Alcott's book, Little Women. The 32x25 oil on canvas was one of a group of illustrations created by Norman Rockwell in 1937 for a serialized biography of Louisa May Alcott in the magazine, Woman's Home Companion. The name of the painting was "Jo Seated on Old Sofa."

"I knew it, I knew it was Jo!" Brenda exclaimed, beaming. "I read Little Women over and over as a little girl growing up in Brooklyn. I used to sit by the front window of our brownstone and read, just like Jo. I was just sort of startled to recognize myself when I came around the corner!" I murmured that I could relate.

Then, dreadlocks swinging, Brenda turned to regard the charcoal sketch on the opposite wall, "Proud Possessor." "Norman Rockwell drew that, too?" she asked. "Yes," I answered, and proceeded to tell her the story of Kiah and Pomp.

Proud Possessor

American Magazine had asked Norman Rockwell to illustrate "Proud Possessor," a short story to appear in its May, 1940, issue. The illustrator knew, almost at once, which scene he would depict.

"Proud Possessor," written by Mississippian James Street and published in 1940, tells the tale of two rural boys–one black, one white–and the two puppies that almost end their friendship. Kiah, the white boy, asks his friend Pomp, the black boy, to care for the pups he's found until he can get his mother to agree to let him keep them. Pomp agrees to care for the dogs (and to keep the matter quiet from Kiah's mom), but only for a stiff payment. When the time comes, Pomp will return the dogs in exchange for Kiah's prized pocketknife.

Norman Rockwell's painting portrays the moment when Kiah, after much internal struggle and external wrangling, agrees to surrender his pride (and his pocketknife) for the love of his animals: he is ready to hand the knife over to the still puppy-clutching Pomp.

ᔓ

The models for "Proud Possessor" were photographed in front of Norman Rockwell's Arlington home. Records indicate that the white boy was Rex P. Sheldon. But thus far, no record of the black model's name has been found.

"Pomp" was definitely not from the Arlington area: no black families were living in that part of Vermont at the time. More likely, the boy came from one of the black families across the Battenkill River in Washington County. It is highly probable that the person who introduced Norman Rockwell to this black model was Grandma Moses.

ଓ

"Norman Rockwell captures the soul of the one he paints. He captures the soul," Brenda Nixon, art therapist, softly declared. "I can feel the whole story, yet he's still leaving room for my own imagination." Another black woman, another epiphany, in another art gallery. All again fueled by the transcendent work, the universal values, of Norman Rockwell.

Feeling The Whole Story

Norman Rockwell's work sparked remembrances and recognition from other people of color that day as well. A Malaysian woman, staring up into a photo portrait of Rockwell, asked, "Is that really his photo? I never saw him." She had grown up seeing Rockwell's illustrations of America, but had never seen the illustrator himself. "Because of him, I decided to come here," she offered. "America looked like a good place. And it is."

Two Mexican-American engineers used their lunch break to tour the exhibit. Rockwell prints were all over the Spanish language calendars in Mexico when they were growing up. Images of the snow-covered New England landscapes were "America *verdad*". The two men commented that they could relate to the "family values" and "feelings of the people" portrayed in Norman Rockwell's paintings. Rockwell's paintings encouraged them: their neighbors to the North might not be so very different from themselves, after all, and they might be able to find a better life there.

Modeling A Better Life

A better life is what Geneitha Welch and Demetria Darling strove to offer their students during forty-plus-years of service in the segregated schools of the South. I met Ms. Welch and Ms. Darling, along with Ms. Darling's son, Walter Miller, while the three were visiting the exhibit, *American Chronicles: The Art of Norman Rockwell* at the Museum of Art in Fort Lauderdale, Florida.

Now a retired art teacher, Geneitha Welch was born in Miami, granddaughter of prominent black business owners of the only drugstore in the segregated Overtown section of the city. When Geneitha was six years old, she moved with her parents to Cleveland, Ohio. The Welches were one of only two black families on the block. Graduating from Spelman College with a degree in art, Geneitha Welch eventually made her way back to Miami.

Demetria Darling, on the other hand, had been born and raised in Bloomington, Indiana. Her father had followed the black migration north from Mississippi to the furniture factory and quarry jobs of Bloomington. Now a retired school counselor, Ms. Darling was the only black child in her elementary school for her first three years. After graduating from the University of Indiana at Bloomington, she eventually found a school counselor position in Miami.

Walter Miller, Ms. Darling's son, was visiting from Bloomington. One reason: he wanted to go to the Rockwell show in Fort Lauderdale.

Walter Miller was not your image of an art museum guest. With his t-shirt and baseball cap, working man's steady gaze and muscular brown forearms, Miller shattered all stereotypes of a typical Norman Rockwell fan.

A self-employed handyman/repairman, Walter Miller had completed a tour of duty with the Marines during the Vietnam War, then used the GI bill to earn a BA in Black History at the University of Indiana. It was while browsing through the University library that he discovered the art of Norman Rockwell–and liked what he saw.

The no-nonsense GI views Rockwell's themes as central and universal: "The sentiments are the same (for black and white). Just the skin color is different." And Walter Miller has surrounded himself with those sentiments: the walls of the home of this Black Studies major are covered with sets of Norman Rockwell plates. The ex-Marine has collected these plates, over the years, from cleaning out garages.

ᔓ

Geneitha Welch and Demetria Darling became fast friends when Darling, school counselor at George Washington Carver Elementary in Miami's historic black community of Coconut Grove, recruited Welch to serve as artist-in-residence at Carver. Both women recalled searching for discarded Norman Rockwell Saturday Evening Post covers to use in lieu of art textbooks for their poorly-supplied classrooms. Both rejoiced that they had lived to see the day they could actually visit Norman Rockwell's work, up close and personal. Both confided to me that they resonated deeply with the themes portrayed in that work.

Reflecting on her childhood in Cleveland, Geneitha Welch studied the little black boy waving from a tree in Norman Rockwell's Saturday Evening Post cover, "Homecoming GI." She observed, "In the beginning, we (black and white) lived in the same communities." "Therefore," Demetria Darling picked up, echoing her son's comments, "the sentiments are the same. We can all relate to them."

I asked the elegantly dressed, silver-haired educator what she thought of the popular wisdom that Norman Rockwell was just about white people. Smiling softly, a knowing twinkle in her eyes, Ms. Darling replied, "When I look for me, I find me."

ꕤ

One of the most profound horrors of racism in America is that, being treated as invisible by whites, blacks can become invisible to themselves. If I only see myself "through the eyes of others," I may not see myself at all. I have to look for me to find me.

Norman Rockwell put people of color into his universal themes of family, community and the coming of age–sometimes explicitly. But this fact is virtually invisible to most white observers. It is seen most clearly through the eyes of the person of color: When I look for me, I find me.

One man whose work has looked for and found black Americans in the universality of Norman Rockwell's themes is the African-American illustrator, Orlando Jewell Black.

A Rockwell Legacy: Orlando Black

"I love me some Norman Rockwell." So states Orlando J. Black, native of Oklahoma City, Oklahoma. That love began when a nine year old Orlando stared up at the Norman Rockwell calendars covering his bedroom wall, and decided he wanted to draw.

The only child of solidly middle class black professionals, those images in the calendar did not seem so far from his own life. Born in 1969, Black reflects: "I grew up in what I like to call 'the glory years,' before we had all these devices that divide us. I had a normal life, a simple life. Because of that, I can relate to Norman Rockwell."

By the time he got to Hoover Middle School, Orlando Black's artistic talent was obvious and his Norman Rockwell attachment evident. "I particularly enjoyed Rockwell's portrayal of children. My favorite back then was his painting of the little boy and girl on a bench with a dog in the back." Again, dedicated public school art teachers stepped up to encourage and develop a talented student. They augmented Orlando's instruction whenever they could, often from Rockwell's *Saturday Evening Post* covers.

Then the young artist discovered Norman Rockwell's "civil rights" paintings. For Black, these works epitomize his definition of an American artist: one who tells a story with a picture. "I love 'Mississippi Justice' for this very reason," Black remarked. "It is complete and clear story telling." "But,", he continued, "I never see it in Rockwell books or on Rockwell calendars. He reached out to an America that many Americans didn't want to see."

In the fall of 1987, Orlando Black enrolled at Oklahoma State University in Stillwater, majoring in graphic design with a minor in fine arts\visual drawing. With his art professors again taking him under special tutelage, the young illustrator concentrated on still life settings and the human form, using the mediums of charcoal, chalk, ink pen and graphite pencil. Often, his sketches were reminiscent of those of his hero during Rockwell's early, pre-photography period.

Black worked at a few graphic arts positions upon leaving Oklahoma State. Then, he received a call to the ministry and went to seminary school. Orlando Black stopped drawing.

In 1997 he married Tiffany Searcy, and in 1999, Black became the fifth full-time pastor of the historic Shiloh Baptist Church, founded in Oklahoma City in 1916. Leading his congregation and raising, with his wife, three energetic sons kept Pastor Orlando from thoughts of art or drawing for twenty years. Then, in 2012, after much prayer, Orlando Jewell Black picked up a graphite pencil and started sketching again. In the past year he has created over forty drawings.

Although Black is receiving an increasing number of requests for formal portraits, his favorite work remains illustrations of children. And his themes are all Rockwell: prayer, play, first loves.

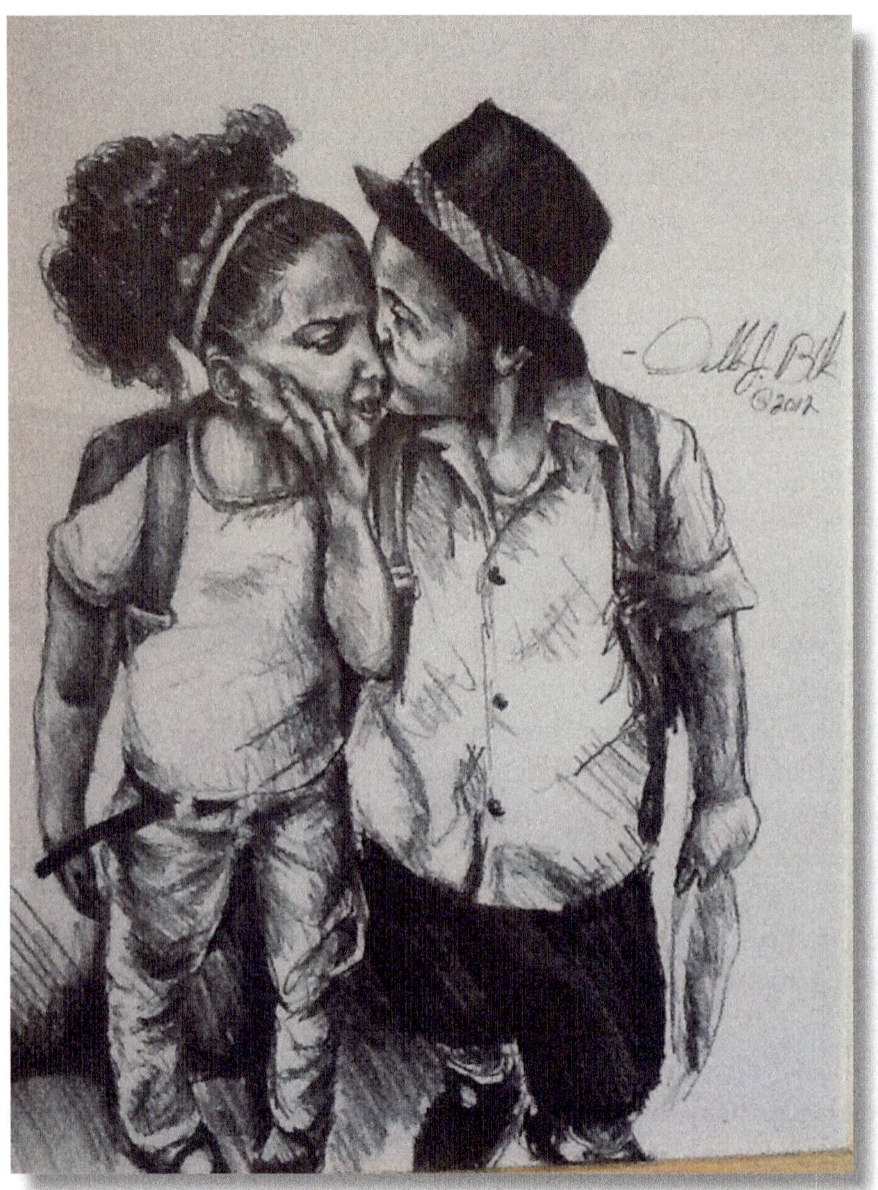

***Puppy Love Smooches* by Orlando J. Black**

In "Puppy Love Smooches," for example, the details of the little lady's ripped pant leg and crinkled brow suggest that she may not be so sure about this sudden transition from tomboy playmate to object of affection. Orlando J. Black is having a heck of a good time telling the stories of his African-American subjects, "Norman Rockwell style."

I can't help but believe that, if he were here to see it, the great illustrator would be very pleased.

ᔓ

Sadly, Norman Rockwell never felt his work made much difference in people's lives. He despaired of having ever produced anything of significance. Yet the fabled illustrator has a living legacy of people whose primary means of art instruction is the studying of his work. Some of these folks might say that Norman Rockwell gave them their careers and their livelihoods. Robin Jordan, the black fashion illustrator from Brooklyn, asserts that, for her, the gift was even greater. Jordan bluntly states: "Norman Rockwell saved my life."

Chapter 10

THE WHITEWASH

"I've got to make money but there ain't nothin' funny about the whitewash."
Jim Wann, composer and songwriter

"We'll be looking for our pictures."
Norman Rockwell models for a *Pan Am Airways* promotion

The colors of ethnic diversity were a part of Norman Rockwell's palette from the earliest days of his career. But almost as soon as they appeared, those colors were muted, almost hidden, under layers of whitewash.

Take the case of the *Pan Am* advertising campaign. When Norman Rockwell took his around-the-world promotional junket for *Pan Am*, he created lots of sketches–not of places, but of "the peoples of the world." In his *My Adventures as an Illustrator*, Rockwell remembers: "Everywhere I went, people asked me, 'What are you sketching for?' 'For advertisements to appear in all the magazines.' I said. Which pleased my questioners no end. 'We'll be looking for our pictures,' they said."

But those models never did see their pictures. Those illustrations were never created. Rockwell returned home to find that the *Pan Am* ad agency didn't want to have anything to do with the "peoples of the world." His sketchbooks were rejected. As far as I know, they never have been published.

Regarding the incident, an embarrassed Rockwell sheepishly admitted, "So now I avoid London, Paris, Barcelona, Rome, Istanbul, Beirut, Karachi, Calcutta, Benares, Rangoon, Bangkok, Hong Kong, Tokyo and Hawaii. If I have any more wide-ranging fiascos like that one I will have to go live in a closet."

When *Pan Am* finally did launch its advertising campaign, a few Rockwell drawings were used, but most of the advertisements depict images of happy tourists on sandy beaches rather than hard working locals on crowded streets. Given the heavy pre-promotion emphasis *Pan Am* had placed on Rockwell's role in the project, most viewers of the ads thought they were seeing "the real Norman Rockwell." But they were not. The real Norman Rockwell had been slapped down, deep-sixed, whitewashed.

Rockwell himself seems to have sensed what was going on. In 1958, he wrote:

"But my worst enemy is the world-shaking idea. Every so often I try to paint the BIG picture, something serious and colossal which will change the world, save mankind. Humor's all right, I say to myself, but if I'm to be remembered I'll have to do something significant, a picture which will reflect the large view, which will have a memorable subject. So I exchange my gentle old back-yard plug for a prancing, majestic stallion and my customary blue work shirt for a coat of shining armor."

But over and over again–as with the United Nations mural, "Glen Canyon Dam" and the *Pan Am* ads–when the illustrator set out to do a "big idea", TPTB (The Powers That Be) would have none of it: ". . . before I know it I'm sprawled on the ground, my nose in the mud, battered and bruised," the artist concludes. "And pretty soon all I've got for my pains is a crick in the neck, a batch of useless photographs, a sheaf of useless sketches."

Even Norman Rockwell's own autobiography has been shaded to fit the desired image. An astute commentator on Deborah Solomon's article in the *New York Times* edition of July 5th, 2010, wrote:

> I teach illustration and fondly recall reading a first edition of Rockwell's autobiography, *My Adventures as an Illustrator*. Rockwell told of his battle with alcoholism. He stated that while others were out doing real things, including fighting wars, he was alone in the studio with his canvas, telling stories, and he began to doubt the worth of his profession. At times, even he found elements of his work saccharine.

> Eventually he came to grips with the value of his life's work and beat his drinking problem. His self-revealing battle with alcohol led me to a greater appreciation of his work. Years later, I went back to the library to share that section of his autobiography with my current students, and found that it is gone from recent editions. His heirs and editors apparently decided to expunge the very part of the autobiography that made Norman Rockwell most human. *Look for an early edition if you want to learn something of the man's courage* (emphasis added).

This first, non- expunged edition of Norman Rockwell's autobiography, published in 1960, is now out of print. A few copies appear to be available from online rare book sellers, with an asking price last time I looked of $350.00. It appears getting "the read" without "the whitewash" does not come cheap.

The Power of Money

Norman Rockwell's life-long values of tolerance and multiculturalism, and the positive outcomes these values supported in the lives of others, are other "humanizing" aspects that have strangely faded from popular wisdom about the artist. From Crystal Malone to John Lane to Orlando Black, Norman Rockwell's "other Americans" have been largely invisible. Why? What purpose could possibly be served by disregarding such a commendable legacy? The answer, simply put, could be money.

From dolls to greeting cards, from soft drinks to bottled water, a multi-million dollar industry has grown up around a particular branding of Norman Rockwell. For example, to celebrate its sixth anniversary, World of Coca Cola, the soda giant's museum located in Atlanta, Georgia, is showing *American Originals: Norman Rockwell and Coca Cola*. The exhibit, which opened in May, 2013, "brings together America's most beloved brand and its greatest illustrator."

The show features three of the six original artworks Coca Cola commissioned from Norman Rockwell during the years 1928 to 1935. "Barefoot Boy," "Out Fishin'" and "Concert on the Steps" capture, according to Ted Ryan, who is the archives director for The Coca Cola Company, "the American spirit and simple moments in life - which is why his (Norman Rockwell's) work is such a great match for Coca Cola".

A great match for Coca Cola. But what about "Love Ouanga" or "Murder in Mississippi"? What about *that* Norman Rockwell? Is he a "great match" with the "simple moments in life" image marketed by the Coca Cola brand? The obvious answer is, "No."

"Rockwell"–the Brand

If you do not wish to imbibe Norman Rockwell Coca Cola, you can drink Norman Rockwell Spring Water, sold at *The Norman Rockwell Museum* and bottled at a local spring in Rockwell's last hometown of Stockbridge, Massachusetts. Fully refreshed, you may then, if you wish, pursue the many opportunities for spending offered by Norman Rockwell "collectibles."

On June 13, 2013, *The Central Pennsylvanian Business Journal* announced that *American Mint*, the Cumberland County-based coin and collectible company, had signed a new license agreement with *Curtis Publishing* for *The Saturday Evening Post* that will allow the company to produce collectibles bearing the paintings of popular 20th-century artist Norman Rockwell. In the press release announcing the agreement, *American Mint* president Kevin Sacher enthuses, "With the new license agreement, we are producing a line of sculpted medallions, pocket watches, collector knives, collector calendars, and collector baseballs in conjunction with *Curtis Publishing*. . . and we are excited to announce this new partnership."

Note the word "collector" in front of each item. Thousands upon thousands of everyday people consider themselves to be "Norman Rockwell collectors". Antonia Piasecki, for example, the Norman Rockwell model who loaned the illustrator her bedroom for his painting, "Road Block," ended her letter to the *Norman Rockwell Museum* with this closing: "I have the "50 Favorites" book and the 1982 ceramic "The Shipmaker" from the N.R. Collectors Club. I am a long-time fan."

Norman Rockwell collectors abound, all apparently ready to lay down hard cash for the next highly valuable piece of Norman Rockwell memorabilia, be it pocket knife or baseball. Will any of these items bear reproductions of "Moving Day" or "The Right To Know" or "Glen Canyon Dam"? Probably not.

Playing Safe With The Brand

In her book, *Out There: Marginalization and Contemporary Cultures,* Michele Wallace observes, "The subject of race, perhaps more than any other subject in contemporary life, feeds on myth." Different segments of society create different myths, different stories about race. These stories often conflict, collide, create controversy.

The continued commercial success of the Norman Rockwell brand, "the simple moments in life," demands that the brand avoid controversy. Race is controversial, no matter how well presented: consider the brouhaha over the bi-racial family in the televised Cheerios ad.

Granted, Hallmark Cards, another Rockwell-brand beneficiary, chose to celebrate the anniversary of its 50-year relationship with Norman Rockwell by casting an African-American actor, Danny Glover, as Shuffleton on their Hallmark Channel made-for-television movie, "Norman Rockwell's Shuffleton's Barbershop." However, as a black barber serving a white clientele in what appears to be an all-white town, Glover's character has confused some white viewers (the figures in Rockwell's original painting, "Shuffleton's Barbershop," are all white) and annoyed many black viewers (the white male protagonist refers to Glover's character as "Uncle Charlie"). The landmines dotting America's racial divide may have claimed another victim.

Thus the safest, most profitable way to manage race in the Norman Rockwell narrative seems to be to ignore it: erase away all the people, places, events, themes, outcomes that might speak to that "universal statement about humanity"–a statement the artist strove to make all his life. ("The little black girl in the white dress" is the exception that supports this rule.)

Well, maybe not erase it away. Just allow it to fade away, fade away under the cover of what African-American Nobel Laureate Toni Morrison calls, "a terrible silence," a silence that can, eventually, commit "an unbearable violence" against the truth.

ᔓ

The United States Postal Service has issued one stamp commemorating Norman Rockwell. Printed in 1972, the stamp shows Rockwell's illustration of Tom Sawyer standing in front of a fence, doing a whitewash.

Epilogue

"If you want to help other people, you have got to make up your mind to write things that some men will condemn."
Thomas Merton, a Trappist monk

"Coincidence is often a messenger sent by Truth."
Jacqueline Winspear, author

ᔕ

When I started writing this book, I had no intention of helping anybody, and no desire to be a messenger of anything. I just thought I'd do a little easy research during the winter, then maybe write a short article or two. Nothing too intense.

But coincidence stepped in. And as it moved me from one piece of the story to the next, I was pushed and nudged towards deeper questions and messier truths. And those truths sobered me: "Nobody believed that I was a Rockwell model. They still don't." "I told him that the figure was a composite of two little girls, but I guess he didn't hear me." "Finally, someone is looking." "I just wanted to do something important." "There ain't nothin' funny 'bout the whitewash."

I am a very different person today than I was that October morning three years ago when Pennie Scales and I stepped into the Norman Rockwell Museum. From the moment I heard my first story from a Rockwell model of color (Pauline Adams Grimes), I promised myself that this book would give name and face and voice to "the others" in Norman Rockwell's America. I was going to be a messenger. I was going to help.

Moreover, as I explored what motivated Norman Rockwell to slip people of color "into the picture" in the first place, I realized there was no "politically polite" way to do this. I was documenting, piece by piece, the famous illustrator's deep commitment to and pointed portrayals of multiculturalism. Up until now, these portrayals have been, as Rockwell biographer Laura Claridge puts it, "bizarrely neglected."

The startling truth is this: as this narrative unfolded, amidst all the voices breaking free, telling their stories for the first time, the loudest voice of all was that of Norman Rockwell. I vowed throughout that I would not "go beyond the data" and/or read too much into things. But over and over, the refrain of my favorite television detective buzzed through my head: "I could be wrong, now. But I don't think so." Writing this book has taken me on a journey more unsettling than I could have ever imaged.

And that journey is far from over. The Navajo models for "Glen Canyon Dam," or at least the descendants of those models, have yet to be specifically identified within the John Lane clan. The black churches in New Rochelle, New York, hopefully can be encouraged to gather oral histories that can identify the people who modeled for "Love Ouanga." Similarly, members of the Chinese community in North Adams may still have stories that can be more fully told about the Asian models in "The Golden Rule." (My dream is that Norman Rockwell's oldest son, Jarvis, an artist in his own right and a resident of North Adams, would help with this.)

I would like to sit down with Robert Cole and learn more about how he and Rockwell worked together. I would love to get Pastor Orlando Black to the Norman Rockwell Museum (he has never been), and maybe even get the institution to create a show of artists of color who have been influenced by Norman Rockwell. I'd like to track down those Norman Rockwell calendars in Malaysia, Mexico and elsewhere and ascertain their influence on perceptions of America.

And the little brown work man, swinging from the top of Norman Rockwell's "Statue of Liberty"? I'd really like to know if President Barack Obama knows he's there.

Finally, my hope is that this book will inspire other Rockwell models of color and their families to step out and tell their stories. The world is listening now, and I trust that now it will believe you.

There is so much more to do, so much more to tell. But I had to get these stories out now, because I promised their tellers I would. The "other people" in Norman Rockwell's America, and the "other Norman Rockwell" himself are not quite so hidden anymore.

About the Author, Jane Allen Petrick

I was told I ought to be a writer way back when I was a fourteen year old freshman at Notre Dame Girls' High School. But I didn't want to hear it. I did not want to be a writer. I did not want the isolation that sets in when a writer gets into "the zone", what the author Mavis Gallant calls "the plunging in (that) frightens me." So I set off to Barnard College and majored in Economics.

But life is what happens when we've made other plans. After completing a doctorate in Organizational Psychology, I established my own consulting practice. One of my clients, who had connections with Addison-Wesley, told the publishing house about my psychological approach to time management. The next thing I knew, I had written and published *Beyond Time Management: Organizing the Organization.*

Then one of my in-laws began dating a staff writer at Ridge Press/ Routledge Books. During a cocktail party, he bemoaned the fact that he had an assignment to write a biography of Otis Redding for young adult readers and he didn't know where to begin. Without thinking (maybe it was the cocktails), I began babbling on about research steps that were, thanks to a good liberal arts education and the gauntlet of earning a doctorate, second nature to me. The next thing I knew, I had a contract with Ridge Press and had written and published *The Otis Redding Story.*

The final confirmation of my destiny to write came with my first "in-house" job as a Ph.D: a corporate directorship with Knight

Ridder, the newspaper syndicate. When the Business Monday editor of *The Miami Herald* asked me, during lunch one day in the staff dining room, about topics for a psychologically healthy workplace column. . . you guessed it. I started babbling again and ended up publishing an article every two weeks for the next four years on the Knight Ridder Newswire.

Three times the charm. I now happily embraces the power of good writing (including, hopefully, *my own* writing) to explain, inform and improve each of our lives. It is my hope that this book has done that for you, and that you have gained as much from reading it as I have learned from creating it for you.

Questions? Comments?

I'd love to hear from you. Post them in the Forums section at the bottom of this book's Amazon page. Just go to www.amazon.com and search for my author's page, Jane Allen Petrick.

If you feel particularly strongly about the contribution this book has made to your understanding of Norman Rockwell and the "hidden" Americans in Norman Rockwell's America, I'd be profoundly grateful if you would post a review of this book in your local newspaper, on Amazon, anywhere you know readers go to get ideas for their next "read".

Finally. . .

If you believe your friends would gain something valuable from *Hidden in Plain Sight: The Other People in Norman Rockwell's America*, I'd be honored if you'd post your thoughts on your social media networks such as Facebook and Twitter.

With my sincerest thanks,

Jane

Selected Bibliography

Berger, Maurice. *For All The World To See: Visual Culture and The Struggle for Civil Rights.* New Haven: Yale University Press, 2010.

White Lies: Race and the Myths of Whiteness. New York: Farrar, Straus, Giroux, 1999.

Claridge, Laura. *Norman Rockwell: A Life.* New York: Modern Library, 2003.

DuBois, W.E.B. *The Souls of Black Folks.* New York: Tribeca Books, 2013.

Edwards, Susan. *NAEA Secondary Teachers.* January 18, 2010. http://naea-secondary-teachers.ning.com/profile/SusanEdwards (accessed July 6, 2013).

Ellison, Ralph. *The Invisible Man.* Vintage, 1995 (2nd. edition).

Fenic, Elsie Wagner. *White Girl in Harlem.* Published by author, limited edition, 2010.

Guyette, Elise. *Discovering Black Vermont: African American Farmers in Hinesburgh, 1790-1890* . University of Vermont Press, 2010.

Halpern, Richard. *Norman Rockwell: The Underside of Innocence.* Chicago: The University of Chicago Press, 2006.

Inside the Saturday Evening Post. June 29, 1946. "Using A Backhand Stroke on the Statue of Liberty. ." June 29, 1946.

Jarman, Rufus. "Profiles: U.S. Artists." *New Yorker Magazine*, March 17, 1945.

Kampfe, John. "Immortalized by Rockwell, Evelyn Hardy Reaches 100." *The Jersey Journal*, March 16, 1983: 1, 49.

Lee, Anthony W. *A Shoemaker's Story: Being chiefly About French Canadian Immigrants, Enterprising Photographers, Rascal Yankees, and Chinese Cobblers in a Nineteenth Century Factory Town.* Princeton, New Jersey: Princeton University Press, 2008.

Life Magazine. "Sorority Fight: Vermont Chapter Stirs Nationwide Controversy By Admitting Negro." May 20, 1946.

Marino, Paul. *Who Is This Guy, Anyway?* n.d. http://paulwmarino.org/who-is-this-guy-anyway.html (accessed September 15, 2011).

Marling, Karal Ann. *Norman Rockwell.* New York: Harry N. Abrams, 1997.

Mead, Rebecca. "Model Student." *New Yorker Magazine*, November 28, 2011: 27.

Memorandum for The Director: Monthly Narrative Report for March for Statue of Liberty National Monument. Superintendent's Monthly Narrative Reports, New York: United States Department of the Interior, National Park Service, 1946.

Meyer, Susan E. *Norman Rockwell's People.* New York: Harry N. Abrams, 1987.

Morrison, Toni. *Playing in the Dark: Whiteness and the Literary Imagination.* New York: Vintage Press, 1993.

Norman Rockwell Museum. *Around The World With Norman Rockwell.* 1955. http://www.youtube.com/watch?v=s6suaItGIPw&list=WLdxywC-uqPGAPAYVjBPrWJ5eC0Y_1a6-T (accessed June 19, 2013).

Norman Rockwell, as told to Tom Rockwell. *My Adventures as an Illustrator.* New York: Harry N. Abrams, 1994.

Paddock, Franklin K. "The Norman Rockwell I Knew." *The Free Library.* JUly 1, 1988. http://www.thefreelibrary.com/The+Norman+Rockwell+I+knew.-a06386114 (accessed June 10, 2011).

Porter, Daniel J. *'Till The Streetlights Came On: Lessons Learned From Neighborhood Games.* Publish Green, 2012.

Rittner, Don. *Troy, NY: A Collar City History.* Arcadia Publishing, 2002.

Ryan, Jim. "Cumberland County-based American Mint to Produce Norman Rockwell Collectibles." *Central Pennsylvania Business Journal,* June 13, 2013.

Saillant, John. *Black Puritan, Black Republican: the Life and Thought of Lemuel Haynes, 1753-1833.* Oxford University Press, 2003.

Schick, Ron. *Norman Rockwell: Behind the Camera.* New York: Little, Brown & Co., 2009.

Smith, Sherry L. and Frehner, Brian (eds.). *Exploitation and Opportunity in the American Southwest.* Santa Fe, New Mexico: SAR Press, 2010.

Solomon, Deborah. "America Illustrated." *New York Times,* July 4, 2010.

Stoeffel, Kate. "Exclusive: Deborah Solomon Out of New York Times Magazine." *The New York Observer,* February 4, 2011.

Wallace, Michelle. "Essay." In *Out There: Marginalization and Contemporary Culture,* by Russell and West, Cornel Ferguson. Cambridge, MA: MIT Press, 1992.

End Notes

Note to the Reader

Solomon, Deborah. "America Illustrated." *New York Times*, July 4, 2010.

Prologue

1 Private correspondence to the author from Laura Claridge, Norman Rockwell biographer.

2 Ellison, Ralph. *The Invisible Man.* Vintage Press, 1995 (2nd. edition).

Chapter 1: Early Glimpses

1 *Life Magazine.* "Sorority Fight: Vermont Chapter Stirs Nationwide Controversy By Admitting Negro." May 20, 1946.

2 Interview with Norman Rockwell. *Esquire Magazine*, January, 1962.

3Marling, Karal Ann. *Norman Rockwell.* New York: Harry N. Abrams, 1997.

4Guyette, Elise. *Discovering Black Vermont: African American Farmers in Hinesburgh, 1790-1890* . University of Vermont Press, 2010.

5 Saillant, John. *Black Puritan, Black Republican: the Life and Thought of Lemuel Haynes, 1753-1833.* Oxford University Press, 2003.

6 Kampfe, John. "Immortalized by Rockwell, Evelyn Hardy Reaches 100." *The Jersey Journal*, March 16, 1983: 1, 49.

7 Rittner, Don. *Troy, NY: A Collar City History*. Arcadia Publishing, 2002.

8 Porter, Daniel J. *'Till The Streetlights Came On: Lessons Learned From Neighborhood Games.* Publish Green, 2012.

9 Fenic, Elsie Wagner. *White Girl in Harlem*. Published by author, limited edition. 2010.

10 Mrs. Merrill was an astute art critic. Norman Rockwell painted his subjects as he found them, big ears and all. Being a woman of a certain age, Mrs. Merrill may have given second thought to being immortalized on the cover of *The Saturday Evening Post.*

11 Letter from Antonia Piasecki to Linda Sackely, then director of the Norman Rockwell Museum. February 11, 1994. Norman Rockwell Archives.

Chapter 2: Hiding in The White House

1 *Memorandum for The Director: Monthly Narrative Report for March for Statue of Liberty National Monument.* Superintendent's Monthly Narrative Reports, New York: United States Department of the Interior, National Park Service, 1946.

2 *Using A Backhand Stroke on the Statue of Liberty.* Inside the Saturday Evening Post. June 29, 1946.

3 Stoeffel, Kate. *Exclusive: Deborah Solomon Out of New York Times Magazine.* The New York Observer. February 4, 2011.

4 Solomon, Deborah. "America Illustrated." *New York Times*, July 4, 2010.

Chapter 3: The Rockwell Models of Washington County

1 Norman Rockwell, as told to Tom Rockwell. *My Adventures as an Illustrator.* New York: Harry N. Abrams, 1994.

2 Ibid.

3 Curtis Publishing Company Website: http://curtispublishing.com/licensing_info.shtml

Chapter 4: Moving On: The Little Black Girl(s) in the Little White Dress

1 Norman Rockwell, as told to Tom Rockwell. *My Adventures as an Illustrator.* New York: Harry N. Abrams, 1994.

2 Robert Coles, *The Story of Ruby Bridges.* New York: Scholastic Press, 1995 [Tells the story of Ruby Bridges' first year of school through words & illustrations; for children, ages 4-8]

3 Katy Reckdahl, "Fifty Years Later, Students Recall Integrating New Orleans Public Schools," *Times-Picayune,(New Orleans, LA), Saturday, November 13, 2010 (with photo gallery).*

4 David Kamp. "Norman Rockwell's American Dream." VanityFair.com. 11/2009.

5 Donald Capps. "Erik H. Erikson, Norman Rockwell, and the Therapeutic Functions of a Questionable Painting." *American Imago.* Summer 2008. Vol. 65, Iss. 2, pg. 191, 38

6 Mead, Rebecca. "Model Student." *New Yorker Magazine*, November 28, 2011: 27.

7 Private correspondence, Philip Maysles to the author.

Chapter 5: The Others in The Golden Rule

1 Norman Rockwell Business Papers Collection. Norman Rockwell Archives, Norman Rockwell Museum. Stockbridge, Massachusetts.

2 Marino, Paul. *Who Is This Guy, Anyway?* n.d. http://paulwmarino.org/who-is-this-guy-anyway.html (accessed September 15, 2011).

3 Lee, Anthony W. *A Shoemaker's Story: Being chiefly About French Canadian Immigrants, Enterprising Photographers, Rascal Yankees, and Chinese Cobblers in a Nineteenth Century Factory Town.* Princeton, New Jersey: Princeton University Press, 2008.

4 Doris C. J. Chu, *Chinese in Massachusetts: Their Experiences and Contributions.* Chinese Culture Institute, 1987

5 Cassandra Orton, "Remembering September 11th". Saturday Evening Post Online, September 11, 2012.

Chapter 6: Modeling the '60's

1 Marling, Karal Ann. *Norman Rockwell.* New York: Harry N. Abrams, 1997.
2 Paddock, Franklin K. "The Norman Rockwell I Knew." *The Free Library.* JUly 1, 1988. http://www.thefreelibrary.com/The+Norman+Rockwell+I+knew.-a06386114 (accessed June 10, 2011).
3 Kirstie L. Kleopfer, "Norman Rockwell's Civil Rights Paintings of the 1960s," Master of Arts Thesis. University of Cincinnati, Department of Art History of the School of Art, College of Design, Architecture, Art & Planning. Cincinnati, Ohio, May 16, 2007.
4 Norman Rockwell Business Papers Collection, Norman Rockwell Archives. Norman Rockwell Museum, Stockbridge, Massachusetts.
5 Jack Doyle. "Rockwell & Race, 1963-1968." *PopHistoryDig.com*, September 22, 2011.
6 Kathi Jaworski. "50 Years Later, the Story of the Peace Corps' Rapid-Fire Start Still Breathtaking." *Nonprofit Quarterly*, September 29, 2011
7 Norman Rockwell, as told to Tom Rockwell. *My Adventures as an Illustrator.* New York: Harry N. Abrams, 1994.
8 Ibid.
9 Norman Rockwell Business Papers Collection, Norman Rockwell Archives, Norman Rockwell Museum, Stockbridge, Massachusetts
10 Richard Reeves, "Norman Rockwell is Exactly Like a Norman Rockwell," *New York Times Magazine,* Sunday, February 28, 1971.

Chapter 7: Coloring The Boy Scouts

1 Claridge, Laura. *Norman Rockwell: A Life.* New York: Modern Library, 2003.
2 Ibid.
3 Ibid.
4 Susan E. Meyer in her book, *Norman Rockwell's People*, also notes, in the final section of the book: "Rockwell was more progressive in his politics than his public might have assumed. He wanted to paint a black Boy Scout, for example, long before such subjects were acceptable to the general public."(p.220)
4 Brown and Bigelow. Boy Scouts: correspondence re: outgoing: Boy Scout calendar complete Norman Rockwell says most complicated in 50 years, says Joe Csatari (Rockwell's Scout paintings assistant and protégé) can make any technical scouting changes, March 13 1973. RC.2007.18.2.29 Text 2
5 Brown and Bigelow. Boy Scouts: correspondence: re: Robert F. Bauer, BoyPOWER campaign: Norman Rockwell endorsement enclosed has helped raise over $12 million and ask for bookmark for his son Keith Bauer, April, 1973. RC.2007.18.2.29 Text 2
6 Jarman, Rufus. "Profiles: U.S. Artists." *New Yorker Magazine*, March 17, 1945.
7 Isaac Crawford, Jr. *Beating the Odds: A Story of Survival.* Xlibris, 2010.

8 Brown and Bigelow: Boy Scouts: correspondence re: outgoing: Norman Rockwell to Joe Csatari. Boy Scout calendar for the Spring 1976 bi-centennial idea, request models in uniform to Stockbridge November 6, 1973. Another letter the same day to Joe allowing him to make changes to Scout painting just delivered enclosed instructions Norman Rockwell was give. 1973. RC.2007.18.2.30 Text 2

9 Norman Rockwell Business Papers Collection, Norman Rockwell Archives, Norman Rockwell Museum, Stockbridge, Massachusetts.

Chapter 8: The Navajos, The Illustrator, and Glen Canyon Dam

1 Rick Antonson. *Route 66 Still Kicks.* Skyhorse Publishing, 2013.

2 Norman Rockwell was so enamored with Hollywood that in 1965 he accepted a bit role as a card player in the movie *Stagecoach*. For the rest of his life, Rockwell paid annual fees to sustain his membership in the Screen Actors' Guild.

3 The Glen Canyon Institute, www.glencanyon.org

4 Stinger, Leslie and Ferguson, Bobby. Portraits of Reclamation. http://www.usbr.gov/museumproperty/art/borart.pdf. 1999

5 Rusho, W. L. (Bud). Oral History Interview. Transcript of tape-recorded Bureau of Reclamation Oral History Interviews conducted by Brit Allan Story, Senior Historian, Bureau of Reclamation, during 1995 in Salt Lake City, Utah. Edited by Brit Allan Storey. Repository for the record copy of the interview transcript is the National Archives and Records Administration in College Park, Maryland.

6 Will Rusho. *Photo of the John Lane Family*. The National Archives.

7 Exploitation and Opportunity in the American Southwest. Edited by Sherry L. Smith and Brian Frehner . SAR Press, 2010. www.sarpress.sarweb.org.

Chapter 9: Norman Rockwell Saved My Life

1 Edwards, Susan. *NAEA Secondary Teachers.* January 18, 2010. http://naea-secondary-teachers.ning.com/profile/SusanEdwards (accessed July 6, 2013).

2 The shape West African men prefer in West African women. For this phrase and definition, I must acknowledge Mma Precious Ramotswe , founder and president of *The Number on Lady Detectives' Agency*.

3 Ellison, Ralph. *The Invisible Man.* Vintage Press, 1995 (2nd. edition).

4 DuBois, W.E.B. *The Souls of Black Folks.* New York: Tribeca Books, 2013.

5 To see a full gallery of Orlando Black's work, go to http://wbpas.org . Click the drop down member tab and select "Orlando Black".

6 Norman Rockwell, as told to Tom Rockwell. *My Adventures as an Illustrator.* New York: Harry N. Abrams, 1994.

Chapter 10: The Whitewash

1 Norman Rockwell Museum. *Around The World With Norman Rockwell.* 1955. http://www.youtube.com/watch?v=s6suaItGIPw&list=WLdxywC-uqPGAPAYVjBPrWJ5eC0Y_1a6-T (accessed June 19, 2013).

2 Norman Rockwell, as told to Tom Rockwell. *My Adventures as an Illustrator.* New York: Harry N. Abrams, 1994.

3 Solomon, Deborah. "America Illustrated." *New York Times,* July 4, 2010.

4 "World of Coca-Cola Displays Largest Exhibit of Norman Rockwell's Work for The Coca-Cola Company." Businesswire.com, May 24, 2013.

5 Ryan, Jim. "Cumberland County-based American Mint to Produce Norman Rockwell Collectibles." *Central Pennsylvania Business Journal,* June 13, 2013.

6 Letter from Antonia Piasecki, Norman Rockwell model, to Linda Sackely, then director of the Norman Rockwell Museum. February

10 Wallace, Michelle. "Essay." In *Out There: Marginalization and Contemporary Culture,* by Russell and West, Cornel Ferguson. Cambridge, MA: MIT Press, 1992.

11 Meyer, Susan E. *Norman Rockwell's People.* New York: Harry N. Abrams, 1987.

12 Morrison, Toni. *Playing in the Dark: Whiteness and the Literary Imagination.* New York: Vintage Press, 1993.

Index

A Special Thank You to the Following Kickstarter Supporters:

Adrian Aoun
Katherine L. Ashton
Mya Bannard
Margarita Benitez
Orlando J. Black
William Burdette
Kimberly Carter
Geoff Cooper
David and Pennie Dell
Amber Drew
Marta Fernandez
Loren and Lilly Frank
Erik Frey
Janet R. Green
Jaclyn Hirsch
David and Diane Hochner
Elana Katz
Robert L. Ladner, Jr.
JoAnn Margolis
Mariza Petrick
Barbara Pickhardte
Joni Primas
Seth Schiesel
Francisco Reisner
LaVergne Trawick
Richard Tyler

CPSIA information can be obtained at www.ICGtesting.com
Printed in the USA
BVOW10s1335111013

333502BV00005B/7/P